BFI TV Classics

BFI TV Classics is a series of books celebrating key individual television programmes and series. Television scholars, critics and novelists provide critical readings underpinned with careful research, alongside a personal response to the programme and a case for its 'classic' status.

Also Published:

Buffy the Vampire Slayer
Anne Billson

Doctor Who
Kim Newman

The Office
Ben Walters

Our Friends in the North
Michael Eaton

Seinfeld
Nicholas Mirzoeff

Seven Up
Stella Bruzzi

The Singing Detective
Glen Creeber

Queer
as Folk

Glyn
Davis

For Iain Telfer Barbour

First published in 2007 by the
British Film Institute
21 Stephen Street, London W1T 1LN

The British Film Institute's purpose is to champion moving image culture in all its richness and diversity across the UK, for the benefiit of as wide an audience as possible, and to create and encourage debate.

Images from *Queer as Folk*, Red Productions; *Queer as Folk 2*, Red Productions; *Queer as Folk US*, Tony Jonas Productions/Cowlip Productions/Temple Street Productions/Channel Four. Page 2 – *The Grand*, Granada Television; p. 9 – *The Naked Civil Servant*, Thames Television; *EastEnders*, BBC; p. 18 – *The League of Gentlemen*, BBC; p. 25 – *Nowhere*, Kill/Desperate Pictures/Blurco/Why Not Productions; p. 46 – *Nighthawks*, Nashburgh/Four Corners Films; p. 60 – *Six Feet Under*, HBO; p. 71 – *Coronation Street*, Granada Television; p. 73 – *The Cops*, BBC; *Shameless*, Company Pictures; p. 106 – *My Own Private Idaho*, New Line Cinema; p. 126 – *Tipping the Velvet*, Sally Head Productions; p. 127 – *Noah's Arc*, Open Door Productions/ Blueprint Entertainment.

Whilst considerable effort has been made to correctly identify the copyright holders, this has not been possible in all cases. We apologise for any omissions or mistakes in the credits and we will endeavour to remedy, in future editions, errors brought to our attention by the relevant rights holder.

None of the content of this publication is intended to imply that it is endorsed by the programme's broadcaster or production companies involved.

British Library Cataloguing-in-Publication Data
A catalogue record for this book is available from the British Library

ISBN 978–1–84457–199–4

Set by Fakenham Photosetting Limited, Fakenham, Norfolk
Printed in the UK by The Cromwell Press, Trowbridge, Wiltshire

Contents

Acknowledgments...vi

Introduction – The Other End of the Ballroom.........1

1 Elephants and Zeppelins...............................22
2 Party Rings, Angel Delight, Nappies................54
3 A Shot to the Head.....................................82
4 Gay as Blazes 110

Notes...129
Credits...132
Index 136

Acknowledgments

I'd like to express my gratitude to the following people for discussing *Queer as Folk*, 'gay telly' and the career of Russell T. Davies with me, and for providing me with invaluable resources and information: Michele Aaron, Pete Bailie, Helen Davis, Jonathan Dovey, Ian Graham, Lucas Hildebrand, Jaap Kooijman, Anna Lau, Andy Medhurst, Paul Smith, Pam Tait and Gregory Woods. At the BFI, I'd like to thank Rebecca Barden and Sarah Watt for their warm support and assistance. Special thanks to those who read earlier versions of the manuscript, and provided detailed and constructive feedback: Kay Dickinson, Alan McKee and Gary Needham.

Introduction

The Other End of the Ballroom

Clive can't find the right words. He's trying to tell his father how he feels, what he is: that he's a homosexual, a queer, that he dances at the other end of the ballroom. Clive's Dad cottons on, and asks his son 'How do you know? ... Where's it come from?'. Stammering, gesturing at his throat and chest, Clive attempts to express himself: 'I dunno. It's *here*. If I knew, I'd cut it out. It's me, and it's not. I don't want it; it's not like I want it. It doesn't stop. It's like it's twisted. It's so strong. I hate it, Dad.'

This scene appears in an episode of *The Grand*, a 1920s-set ensemble-cast television drama about the comings and goings of the eponymous hotel. The programme, which was produced by Granada for ITV, ran for two series (1997–8), eighteen episodes in total, and was entirely written by Russell T. Davies. Clive's story may seem familiar – the clumsy and painful coming out of a gay character, the unhappy homosexual who wishes he wasn't – but it was nevertheless an important landmark in Davies's career. For not only was it the first time that he created and fleshed out a believable gay character (admittedly, there were some pseudo-lesbian Nazis in his earlier BBC children's drama *Dark Season* (1991), although they never openly admitted as much), but it was this episode of *The Grand* that secured him the job of writing *Queer as Folk*.

Queer as Folk was first screened on Channel 4 in 1999, and is often referred to by critics and academics as 'groundbreaking', even 'revolutionary'. Crucially, it was the first fictional television programme in which almost all of the main characters were gay or lesbian. Set in Manchester, the series followed the adventures of sci-fi fan Vince Tyler (Craig Kelly), his sexually voracious best pal Stuart Jones (Aidan Gillen) and new kid on the scene Nathan Maloney (Charlie Hunnam). *Queer as Folk* was swiftly identified as a landmark television series, 'hailed', according to journalist Rob Brown, 'as an instant classic by almost everyone'.[1] Stuart Millar and Janine Gibson, writing in the *Guardian* the day after the broadcast of the first episode, referred to the programme as 'a milestone in the battle for sexual equality'; Alistair Pegg, the editor of the *Pink Paper*, said that 'The show is probably the best representation we have seen of ordinary gay lives on television.'[2] Megan Radclyffe in *Gay Times* stated that 'the series is definitely a landmark. Not only is it realistic, but the portrayals are utterly believable, the soundtrack is fucking sublime ..., and the dark lighting is just the right side of lascivious. This is the full-on queer version of *This*

2

Clive from *The Grand*

Life we've all been craving …'[3] In *Time Out*, Alkarim Jivani wrote that *Queer as Folk* was 'a huge advance in the televisual depiction of gay life', and Rupert Smith even dubbed Russell T. Davies 'the Jacqueline Susann of gay Manchester'.[4]

Unapologetically ignoring debates about 'positive images', *Queer as Folk* had both empathetic and reprehensible queer characters – as well as some who managed to be both. It depicted the hedonism of gay bar and club culture, while also highlighting that scene's homogeneity. Seemingly designed to cause heated discussion, the programme's roster of characters included lesbian parents, homophobic schoolboys and bi-curious businessmen, and the series featured ribald language and frequent scenes of nudity and sex. Indeed, the show provoked considerable controversy on its initial airing: in particular, the first episode's scene of a teenage boy having sex with a man in his late twenties caused switchboards to light up with complaints from irate viewers. However, the series was a significant critical and commercial success: not only did Channel 4 subsequently commission a second series – *Queer as Folk 2* – which it aired in 2000, but the show's premise was sold to the US, where a remade and significantly expanded version, also called *Queer as Folk*, ran on the cable channel Showtime for five seasons.

3

Aside from its depiction of queer characters and culture – which I will return to shortly – *Queer as Folk* was a pivotal programme in the history of British television drama, and thus worthy of being dubbed a 'television classic', for a variety of reasons. First, it made Russell T. Davies a recognisable name in television-writing. Born in Swansea in 1963, Davies studied English Literature at Oxford University, graduating in 1984. He initially worked as a floor manager and production assistant for the BBC, before taking the corporation's in-house directing course in the late 1980s. He followed this with several years working in children's television at the BBC: a one-off appearance in front of the camera on *Play School*, several years behind the scenes of magazine programme *Why Don't You …?*, some sketch-show writing for *Breakfast Serials* and *ChuckleVision*. Davies then wrote, and had commissioned, two six-part science-fiction/fantasy drama serials for children's BBC, *Dark Season* and *Century Falls* (1993). In 1992, Davies began working for Granada as a producer and writer on the ITV children's hospital drama *Children's Ward* (1989–2000). While working on that programme, he also wrote for some of Granada's adult series, including the daytime soap *Families* (1990–3) and the comedy *The House of Windsor* (1994); additionally, he worked as a storyliner for *Coronation Street*. *The Grand* was his first large commission, and the series was a ratings success, playing at its peak to audiences of 11 million. Davies's work after *Queer as Folk*, including *Bob and Rose* (Red for ITV, 2001), *The Second Coming* (Red for ITV, 2003), *Mine All Mine* (Red for ITV, 2004), *Casanova* (BBC, 2005) and the relaunch of *Doctor Who* (BBC, 2005–), has been both critically lauded and commercially successful. Along with Paul Abbott – *Clocking Off* (Red for BBC, 2000–3), *State of Play* (Endor/BBC, 2003), *Shameless* (Company for Channel 4, 2004–) – Davies is often seen as one of the most consistently interesting and exciting writers working in British television today; critic Mark Lawson has even compared Davies with Dennis Potter, due to the ability both writers have had for arousing controversy.[5]

Second, *Queer as Folk* was the first programme commissioned by Nicola Shindler's Red Production Company. Shindler – born in Rochdale in 1968 and educated at Cambridge University (where she swapped from Law to History) – originally wanted to become a theatre director. But after working in publicity at the Royal Court Theatre, she moved into television. Shindler quickly made a name for herself by working on several high-profile 'quality' drama projects: she was a script editor for *Cracker* (on the story 'To Say I Love You', produced by Granada for ITV, 1993), an assistant producer on *Our Friends in the North* (BBC, 1996), an associate producer of *Prime Suspect 5* (also known as *Errors of Judgment*; Granada for ITV, 1996) and a producer on Jimmy McGovern's docudrama *Hillsborough* (Granada for ITV, 1996). Shindler ventured out on her own in 1998 to form Red – named after her favourite football team, Manchester United, 'The Red Devils'.

4

Russell T. Davies

5

The company was established in Manchester deliberately – 'I really like things with a regional voice. Regardless of what it is, they're less bland'[6] – and swiftly garnered a reputation for quality (and controversy) with *Queer as Folk*. Red's subsequent output, which has included *Clocking Off* and *The Second Coming*, has contributed significantly to what some critics have seen as a recent renaissance in British television drama.[7]

Third, *Queer as Folk* was an important series for Channel 4. Launched in November 1982, Channel 4's broadcast charter included a remit to experiment and innovate in both form and content, as well as to provide for those audiences neglected by the other terrestrial channels. This produced a roster of imaginative programming in the station's first decade, including a notable commitment to television for minority audiences. Lesbian and gay viewers were catered for with, among other things, screenings of several Derek Jarman movies in 1985, a season of films entitled *In The Pink* (1986) and the lesbian and gay magazine programme *Out on Tuesday* (1989–90), later retitled *Out* (1991–2).[8] If the channel's commitment to minorities had waned during the 1990s – due in part to commercial pressures to compete for audience share – the commissioning and screening of *Queer as Folk* seemed to clearly signal Channel 4's political positioning within the landscape of British broadcasting, and reconnected the station to its own history. Indeed, Chris Higgins, writing in *Gay Times*, called *Queer as Folk* 'the sort of programme that we always felt Channel Four should provide, but which it's never delivered'.[9] However, this recognition of the channel's courage and commitment to supporting and airing the series needs to be tempered by the fact that Channel 4 was urgently seeking some critical and commercial success. Ratings analyst William Phillips noted in February 1999 that the channel desperately needed to invest in drama franchises: 'Channel 4 … started 1998 very weakly with their worst peak-time start for seven years and this week, yet again, the five most popular shows on Channel 4 have been editions of [genteel afternoon quiz show] *Countdown*.'[10] In addition, 1999 was the first year in which Channel 4 was solely responsible for selling its own airtime: when launched in 1982, an agreement was struck that Channel 4's commercial breaks would be sold to advertisers by ITV in order to protect the new company financially, and to enable it to focus on producing innovative new programming. In 1999, then, Channel 4 had to prove its independent commercial viability to advertisers. In order to do this, it needed instances of flagship 'quality' output, one of which was *Queer as Folk*.

Finally, beyond the realm of television broadcasting, *Queer as Folk* also marked a significant intervention in queer politics in Britain. In 1999, when the series first aired, Tony Blair's 'New Labour' government had been in power in the UK for two years, and yet many of the electoral promises they had made to Britain's queer citizens had failed to materialise in any form. *Queer as Folk* explicitly narrativised some of the political issues continuing to affect lesbians and gay men in Britain in the late 1990s (queer parenting rights, the age of consent, workplace homophobia, the legal standing of same-sex couples) and thus reminded its viewers of the unequal status afforded to non-heterosexual individuals in the UK. More than this, however, by operating as a controversial 'flashpoint' in British popular culture, the series worked as a polemical argument for political change and its impact thus extended beyond its regular core audience. Images from the series, for instance, were used in the press to accompany articles and essays about the status of contemporary British queer politics.[11] In this sense, *Queer as Folk* can be read as an important landmark in the history of political British television drama, a lineage which would include *Cathy Come Home* (BBC, 1967) and *Boys from the Blackstuff* (BBC, 1982). This connection between representation and political significance was made by Duncan Marr, in an article written for *Gay Times*:

> It is possible, when you're tackling a contentious subject, to be ground-breaking simply by telling it like it is, because it's never been said before. Think Ken Loach (*Cathy Come Home*), or Alan Clarke (*Made in Britain*), just with added jeeps and jokes. Is it such a radical thought that there are 15-year-old boys who know that they're gay and who are driven to find men to have sex with? You knew it and I knew it, but we can't be ground-breaking in private, and Davies added the crucial little detail of saying it out loud and convincingly.[12]

7

* * *

Queer as Folk, as already noted, is historically significant as the very first television drama series in which almost all of the main characters were gay or lesbian. Across the decades of British television history, queer people and characters have, of course, proliferated. As Andy Medhurst identifies,

> there have ... been thousands of images purporting to depict us, in every available genre and at all points of the schedule, from well-meaning liberal drama to crassly reductive sitcom, from *Kilroy* debates on lesbian

motherhood to Hinge and Bracket appearing on the women's team in *Give Us a Clue*.[13]

In addition to this range of images, queer television audiences have also been able to search out for themselves 'stolen pleasures', incidental moments in individual programmes captured for personal, solitary pleasure: the exposure of flesh, the suggestive and titillating interpersonal frisson, the erotic potential of a same-sex locale. Medhurst calls these 'snatched glances':

> what we learnt to cultivate … were two specifically attuned senses: first a lightning-fast freeze-frame memory that glued key images into our minds, and secondly a keen nose for scenting out which programmes would be likely to deliver such treasures. Perhaps this was where we learnt to cruise, scavenging through the schedules, scouring and decoding the *Radio Times* for the slight but telling clue.[14]

Over the years, then, British queer audiences might have been attaining a great deal of pleasure from TV – from specific lesbian and gay roles and performers (even if they weren't always overtly named as such), from stolen moments, from reading against the grain, as well as other sorts of satisfactions afforded by television to all consumers (companionship, debate, knowledge, storytelling, and so on). But in the realm of television drama, the actual number of openly lesbian or gay characters was small, and sorely limited in its range. The avoidance of stereotypes was rare, and queer characters, if not being used as comic relief, often ended up dead or unhappy. The 1975 television film *The Naked Civil Servant* (Thames for ITV) stands out as an extraordinary counter-example; based on the autobiography of Quentin Crisp, it not only depicted aspects of British queer culture (cruising, bars) rarely seen on television, but it placed a queer character centre-stage, and portrayed him in a sympathetic manner. Indeed, Rupert Smith has noted that the film offered 'challenging, rounded examinations of sexuality' not seen again on British television 'until … *Queer as Folk* came along in 1999'.[15]

During the 1980s and 1990s, as the gay rights movement gathered momentum and visibility in the UK, television drama responded by occasionally incorporating bland, inoffensive 'positive images' of homosexuality: asexual, morally upright characters whose mundane 'normality' prevented them from having much depth or life. Colin Russell (played by gay actor Michael Cashman) was introduced into *EastEnders* in 1986; in 1994, Della and Binnie became the first lesbian couple to appear in the soap. Same-sex kisses were usually controversial, as the snog between Beth and her girlfriend Margaret in *Brookside* demonstrated in 1993. At the time of *Queer as Folk*'s broadcast, the most prominent gay and lesbian characters appearing on television were the vet Zoe Tate (Leah Bracknell) in *Emmerdale*, staff nurse Sam Colloby (Jonathan Kerrigan) and bed-manager Adam Osman (Pal Aron) in *Casualty*, and Simon (Andrew Lynford) and Tony (Mark Homer) in *EastEnders*. The latter couple were a spur in Davies's writing of *Queer as Folk*:

> I think they helped me a great deal, those two, because I'd watched all that ... and it gave me the clearest guideline of what not to write. I sat there incensed – well, actually, I couldn't even be bothered to be incensed, I'm lying, I was so bored by it. And the episodes where they'd broken up and Simon goes to Soho to a gay bar to meet his friends and they all sit –

9

The Naked Civil Servant

Simon and Tony from *EastEnders*

sit around a shiny table and – in a chrome bar and talk about – and literally they end up talking about AIDS and the effects of combination therapy on the body system, you know, for AIDS sufferers and stuff like that, and it is just the most execrable scene I've ever seen in my life. It's the lowest, lowest moment of 'gay drama' in inverted commas and it's shocking.[16]

And yet there were signs that some sectors of the television audience might accept alternative depictions of gay and lesbian characters: more rounded individuals who weren't entirely sanitised or always morally correct. Channel 4 financed an adaptation of Armistead Maupin's novel *Tales of the City* in 1993. Although the story centred around the adventures of a straight female character, Mary Ann Singleton (Laura Linney), the San Francisco-set drama was populated with lesbians, bisexuals, gay men and transsexuals. Although queer sex mostly occurred off-screen, at least it was evidently happening, in contrast to the lack of passion in *EastEnders*' Albert Square. And in *This Life* (World Productions for BBC, 1996–7), Warren Jones (Jason Hughes), though the only gay housemate in a gang of five, talked openly about his sexuality and had a great deal of (graphically depicted) sex. Although Warren was in counselling – the first episode of the series began with him talking to his therapist – so were most of his flatmates. The sex that Warren had was depicted in the same manner as that of his heterosexual counterparts: as messy, noisy and occasionally funny writhing.

* * *

A number of different people were responsible for the germination, development and commissioning of *Queer as Folk*, including Russell T. Davies, Nicola Shindler, newly appointed Channel 4 Heads of Drama Gub Neal and Catriona MacKenzie, and Channel 4 executive Michael Jackson. This is a vital point. *Queer as Folk* is usually associated with Davies, in part because he multitasked as the series' creator, writer and co-producer, in part because he took on the largest amount of publicity about the series, but also due to the fact that television drama remains a writer's medium, with programmes often marketed to audiences through their authors. However, the production of any television programme is always a collaborative project: if this book repeatedly draws on quotes by Davies, this is simply because they are so widely available, and other personnel associated with *Queer as Folk* were not interviewed as frequently.

MacKenzie and Neal, both formerly at Granada, had crossed paths with Shindler on specific drama productions she had worked on, including *Cracker*, *Prime Suspect* and *Hillsborough*; they were aware that she was starting up her own Manchester-based production company. It was MacKenzie who approached Davies in late 1997: she had been impressed by the 'Clive' episode of *The Grand* and wanted Davies to write a new drama series for Channel 4. She told him to 'go gay' and initially suggested the possibility of a gay flatshare show – a queerer version of *This Life*, perhaps, which Davies has sardonically noted could have been called something like *That's My Muesli!*.[17] Unemployed at the time, Davies jumped at the chance. Originally, he planned to write the definitive piece of gay television by depicting all the rainbow colours of the queer world, including older gay men, HIV-positive individuals, fag-hags, drag queens and trannies:

> I went away and thought about it, and thought, oh, we'll have two lesbians, and we'll have an older gay man and, and … you know, I was imagining covering the whole community, you know, laughably, like you could ever do that. But in my first thoughts there was a representative of everyone. And then of course you sort of realize that oh, my god, they're just representative, they are dull and the more you can focus it, the better it's going to be.[18]

Elements of this desire to be representative remained in the final version of *Queer as Folk*, in the peripheral characters – Hazel's lodger Bernie, the sidelined lesbian couple Lisa and Romey, and so on. But the decision to focus in on a central couple, Stuart and Vince, was crucial in the development of the series. As Davies tells it:

11

I fixed on a story I'd always wanted to tell, regardless of sexuality: two best friends, one secretly in love with the other. God, the times I've met that pair. The times I've been one of them. That was crystallised late in 1997 when I met this exact couple in Manchester's Cruz 101. One boy was beautiful; his little friend was not, and was therefore funnier and chattier, while always doting on the beauty at his side. And for all the secrecy, somehow they both knew what was going on, but would never say it aloud. They'd been like this since they were fourteen. They needed each other, completed each other, and maybe even destroyed each other. [. . .] I wonder if they're still together?[19]

This 'unrequited love' narrative thus became the vital, emotional heart of *Queer as Folk*. In this regard, it is worth comparing the series with other television programmes featuring similar dynamics: the poignant Niles/Daphne relationship in early seasons of *Frasier* (Grub Street Productions/Paramount for NBC, 1993–2004), or the pining of Ross for Rachel in the first few years of *Friends* (Bright/Kauffman/Crane Productions/WB for NBC, 1994–2004). The universality of this tale ensured the appeal of *Queer as Folk* beyond a niche gay market – indeed, the main audiences for the series were gay men and young heterosexual women.[20]

Ultimately, then, the decision to focus in on Stuart and Vince – and the disruption caused to their relationship by the arrival of Nathan – ensured the success of *Queer as Folk*. But this choice came at a cost: despite the praise and viewing figures that the programme garnered, criticisms were levelled against it for *not* being representative of all of gay life in Britain. Queer critics and commentators, acting as cultural gatekeepers, were nervous and concerned about the messages that the series sent out to the wider audience: what was this show saying about contemporary queer life in Britain? The show was lambasted for focusing almost exclusively on young, white, clubbing-and-sex-obsessed gay men, for pushing lesbian characters to the margins, and for not featuring discussions about AIDS and safe sex. Angela Mason, the director of the gay rights group Stonewall, argued that *Queer as Folk* 'certainly didn't challenge any stereotypes. All the gay men wanted to have non-stop sex and all the lesbians wanted babies. I thought the explicit sex scenes with a youthful 15-year-old did smack of sensationalism.'[21] Pop star Boy George wrote in the *Sunday Express* that

> Sadly, gays on TV are either portrayed as fluffy and inoffensive or ruthless and imbalanced. What I want to see is a balanced view of gay culture. *Queer as Folk* is about as balanced as Myra Hindley and where does it take us in the struggle for equality, and more importantly, understanding?[22]

A letter to *Time Out* from reader David Smith claimed that 'Davies' programme, like the scene that it wallows in, shows absolutely no sign of updating a stereotyped image of gay people as selfish, hollow body-fascists. Thanks, Russell: you've just confirmed to every homophobe in Britain what they thought all along.'[23] In interview after interview, the production team had to defend the series. 'This is a very, very narrow

Vince and Stuart: unrequited romance

slice of gay life', Davies told the *New York Times*; 'To criticize it for not depicting everyone is like watching a current-affairs documentary and saying, "Why isn't there more cookery?" '.[24] He directly took on queer critics in a short piece written for the British gay magazine *Attitude*:

> When this all began in November 1997, no one told me there was an agenda. Because there must be an agenda – every gay politician, spokeswoman and militant has shouted at me for not following it. Perhaps it's available in public libraries, or Clone Zone. I don't know – I never looked.[25]

And he was still defending his decisions during interviews for *Queer as Folk 2*, by which time he had become even more belligerent and vituperative:

> My favourite response to the first series is the people who came up saying 'I've lived with my boyfriend for ten years and *we* go to the opera and have dinner parties, why don't you write about *that*?' And I say, 'Oh, that's *interesting*.' Hello! I write drama, not fucking dreary bollocks, like your life is. Fuck off.[26]

One of the 'problems', of course, was that the three lead characters in *Queer as Folk* were unashamedly not 'positive images'. They were not designed, as Andy Medhurst puts it of Colin from *EastEnders*, 'for gay men's anxious parents and for A-level media studies teachers to show their students that there are some perfectly nice men who, hey, just happen to be gay'.[27] Indeed, Davies smartly recognised that debates about representation had moved on. And so had the tastes of audiences: a significant percentage of Channel 4's audience were prepared to stomach stories featuring complex queer characters. Stuart, Vince and Nathan would behave at times in selfish and unsympathetic ways; their lives included casual drug use and plentiful nights of drinking and dancing; 'messages' and speechifying – like the *EastEnders* discussions about AIDS – were almost entirely absent from the series. Gub Neal defended the focus and the tone of *Queer as Folk*:

Most of the gay drama we've had on British television has dealt with big statements: victimization, the political agenda, AIDS … But this group of characters doesn't think they're victims at all. They're not even aware that they're a minority. They simply exist and say, 'Hey, we don't have to make any apologies, and we're not going away.' The series has given us a chance to simply reveal gay life, to some extent, in its ordinariness. [. . .] There's never been anything that was this explicit or graphic or sustained in its depiction of gay characters … We've come a long way when every gay character on television doesn't have to be a positive stereotype.[28]

It is vital to note that this really was the first time such an approach to depicting queer characters had been taken. *Queer as Folk* offended some people, but it was testing and troubling the acceptable limits of television representation. In order to make progress in a society's attitudes towards hot political and cultural topics – such as sexuality – it is sometimes necessary to go a little too far, to say things that people might not want to hear, to provoke debate.

15

* * *

A brief aside about that title. Davies toyed with a number of possibilities for *Queer as Folk*: at one point, it was known as 'The Other End of the Ballroom', at another as *Queer as Fuck*. The final title chosen brought together two distinct meanings: the English use of the phrase 'There's nowt as queer as folk' to mean 'Aren't people strange?', a comment often associated with northerners (and thus appropriate to the series' Manchester setting); and a play on the phrase 'queer as fuck', a slogan seen on the T-shirts and posters of various activists working for queer politics, especially in North America.

Although the term 'queer' has been used to mean 'strange' for centuries, it gained an association with sexual deviance in the late nineteenth century that has persisted to date. Almost always used pejoratively throughout the twentieth century, a move was made in the late 1980s and early 1990s to reclaim the term. In a manner similar to some black cultures reclaiming the word 'nigger', various non-straight groups and individuals – and it is crucial to note that the term is used, inclusively, to forge links across genders and non-normative sexual orientations – began to use 'queer' to refer to themselves, to mobilise it as a badge of identity. To call oneself 'queer' was to counteract the negative connotations of the term (oddness, perversity, marginality, abjection), to give those associations an alternative valence, and to revel in them. 'Queer' was differentiated from 'lesbian and gay': it included both of those labels, but was more expansive, also used to include bisexuality, transsexuality, other atypical sexualities, sexual deviants of all races, ethnicities, nationalities, classes and abilities, and so on. Where lesbian and gay politics might, traditionally, have been seen as assimilationist, working to carve out an acceptable niche in a straight world, queer politics were often more confrontational and radical, as with the activities of groups like Queer Nation in the US or OutRage! in the UK.

Queer cultural production gathered momentum during the 1990s: the output of a number of film-makers was branded 'New Queer Cinema' by the critic B. Ruby Rich, and in music a number of punky guitar bands (Fifth Column, Sister George, Pansy Division) united under the label 'Queercore'.[29] Using the word 'queer' in the title of a television programme was a bold and provocative move: it was the first time that this had been done (only the cartoon *Queer Duck* [Mishmash Media for Showtime, 1999] and reality makeover show *Queer Eye for the Straight Guy* [Scout/Bravo, 2003–] have followed suit). Using the term not only allied *Queer as Folk* to a broader social movement of disruption and 'independent' countercultural activity, but it introduced some of the elements of that scene into a mainstream medium, beamed into homes across the nation.

* * *

The first script produced by Davies in February 1998 was way too long. With the assistance of Matt Jones – like Davies, an alumni of the British soap scene and a committed fan of *Doctor Who* – this draft was cut in

16

half, and became the first two episodes of the series. It was this material that was accepted and greenlighted by Channel 4. The series was given a budget somewhere in the region of £3 million. Two directors were recruited: Charles McDougall, who had previously worked with Shindler as the director of *Hillsborough*, would helm the first four episodes; Sarah Harding, who had directed instalments of *The Grand* (including the Clive episode), would take the second half. Filming of the first season of *Queer as Folk* took place between 31 August and 19 December 1998. Articles about – and publicity for – the series began to appear during those months, with Britain's gay press (*Attitude*, *Gay Times*, the *Pink Paper*) all invited on set to witness and report on the filming. Other crucial queer cultural events and moments took place during the shooting of *Queer as Folk*. In the United States, twenty-two-year-old student Matthew Shepard was killed in October 1998: attacked on the night of the 6th, he died from his injuries on the 12th. In the UK, on Saturday 5 December, George Michael appeared on *Parkinson* to give his first full interview following his arrest for cottaging; the programme was watched by almost 8 million people.

17

In addition to *Queer as Folk*, the new year's television schedule in 1999 witnessed the appearance of a number of gay/queer television programmes. The first series of Jonathan Harvey's sitcom *Gimme Gimme Gimme* (made by Tiger Aspect for the BBC), about a very camp actor (James Dreyfus) sharing a flat with a brash working-class cockney (Kathy Burke), began screening on Friday 8 January on BBC2. Comedy series *The League of Gentlemen* made the transfer from Radio 4 to BBC2, first showing on 11 January: in addition to its roster of sexually deviant characters – including mid-op transsexual Babs, of Babs' Cabs – the all-male cast were, a little like the Pythons, not averse to donning drag (and the more grotesque, the better). On Thursday 18 January, the dating show *Dishes* on Channel 4 – on which potential partners had to cook for each other – featured a one-off gay episode. And on Wednesday 10 February, Channel 4 began broadcasting the US series *Sex and the City* (Darren Star Productions/HBO, 1998–2004): created by a gay man, Star, and featuring a number of queer characters

The League of Gentlemen

and plotlines, the series was identified by some critics as featuring women who talk and act more like gay men than 'real women'.[30]

The first episode of *Queer as Folk* was broadcast on Tuesday 23 February: although initially scheduled for 10pm, Channel 4 shunted the programme into a 10.30pm slot at the last minute, broadcasting an episode of *Father Ted* at 10pm instead. In terms of the terrestrial landscape, the first instalment was scheduled against the documentary *Workers at War* (BBC1), *Newsnight* (BBC2), a programme about young footballers on ITV called *The World at Their Feet*, and the film *Johnny Mnemonic* (five). Regarding its success with audiences, *Queer as Folk* drew around 2.5 million viewers for its first episode, with a further 1.3 million watching the Saturday-night repeat. Added together, this makes for a 17 per cent audience share – significantly larger than Channel 4's usual average of about 10 per cent. There were claims in the *Pink Paper* that up to 750,000 viewers switched off or over before the end of the first episode, but these were denied by Channel 4.[31] Throughout the first series, ratings held fairly steady at around 2.3 million for the Tuesday broadcast, and 1 million for the weekend repeat.

18

The peak of publicity for *Queer as Folk* occurred in the week before and the week after the broadcast of the first episode. However, commentary and criticism continued during the airing of the series, and Channel 4 had to manage incidents involving corporate supporters, industry watchdogs and lobby groups. Beck's Beer, sponsors of the screening of *Queer as Folk*, withdrew their support after just two episodes. Their logo, which appeared before and after every chunk of the drama, simply vanished. Beck's claimed that they needed to cut their advertising budget, but Russell T. Davies called their withdrawal 'a homophobic response'.[32] In addition, the Independent Television Commission, which monitors British broadcasting, received 163 complaints in total about the first series of *Queer as Folk*. In the ITC's history, only Channel 4's screening in 1995 of Martin Scorsese's film *The Last Temptation of Christ* (1988) caused more controversy. Janine Gibson, writing in the *Guardian*, related the ITC's response to viewers' grievances about *Queer as Folk*:

> Although the ITC did not uphold the complaints about homosexual activity, the regulator had 'concerns about the celebratory tone' of the first episode which, it said, 'left little room for any questions to be raised in viewers' minds about the rights and wrongs of the illegal under-age relationship'. Channel 4 was also censured for failing to take the opportunity to provide educational back-up to the series on subjects such as safe sex, and young people and sexuality. Further episodes of the series should be 'enhanced by such responsible messages.'[33]

19

And to add further to their woes, Channel 4's offices in London were picketed in March 1999 by a few individuals from a group called International Third Position, which was established by former members of the National Front. ITP handed out leaflets ('Channel 4 – Queer Scum') which criticised Channel 4 for 'pushing overtly homosexual propaganda' and stated that *Queer as Folk* 'glorifies sodomy'.[34]

Significant gay news made the press during the months that *Queer as Folk* was shown. On 1 March, the Sexual Offences

(Amendment) Bill, which would equalise the age of consent for heterosexuals and homosexuals at sixteen, successfully made it through the House of Commons. Bisexual pop star Dusty Springfield died on 2 March. On 3 March, footballer Graeme Le Saux accused fellow player Robbie Fowler of a 'gay smear'; during a match Fowler had publicly suggested, via a none-too-subtle gesture, that Le Saux was queer. Also in March of 1999, a news story about the Bolton Seven – a group of men arrested and convicted for taking part in 'sex parties', one of whom was seventeen at the time – continued to rumble on, even though their court case had taken place in February 1998. On the day that the final episode of *Queer as Folk* was first screened, Tuesday 13 April – and as if to contribute to the unhappiness that queer fans might feel at the series coming to a close – the Sexual Offences (Amendment) Bill was sabotaged in the House of Lords. This list, considered alongside the rash of new 'queer TV' programming that appeared in the first months of 1999, suggests a notable visibility and currency for homosexuality in Britain at this time – part of what some commentators have called the 'mainstreaming of homosexuality', a topic I will return to later.

* * *

The first chapter of this book focuses on episodes one to four of *Queer as Folk*, Chapter 2 on episodes five to eight. Chapter 3 explores the sequel, *Queer as Folk 2*, and the final chapter discusses the US remake of the series. Charting a chronological path through the development of the programme enables sustained examination of the production history of the series in the order it unfolded. Within each chapter, themes and topics of discussion are extricated from individual episodes for exploration. My aim throughout is to highlight the textures and pleasures of *Queer as Folk* (its aesthetics, narrative strategies, challenges to the history of 'gay TV', and so on) and their significance, as well as to identify the unique contributions of the series to the history of television drama. In my analysis, I repeatedly return to the politics of the programme, assessing the import, relevance and resonances of specific scenes, images, characters, stretches of dialogue and so on. It is important to note that this is my particular emphasis, and may not be one that squares comfortably with the professed aims and intentions of the series' creative personnel. That is, producers and writers of television drama are regularly more concerned – at least according to their public statements – with creating successful characters, stories, arcs, involvement and entertainment, than with sloganeering or conveying 'messages'. Having said this, Russell T. Davies has, in retrospect, identified the political significance of *Queer as Folk*:

> You know, if you had a camera on me sitting here when I was writing it, then I would have gone no, no, no, it's not [political] at all. And actually that shows how naïve I was in a way. But once it hit transmission, it only then became absolutely clear to me that just the simple act of writing about gay men in the twentieth century is a political act. It is, our lives are political, whether we like it or not – our existence is a political thing. So it's certainly the most political thing I've ever written, without ever once thinking about it in terms of a political drama, I never did that.[35]

21

1 Elephants and Zeppelins

In a scene that was cut from *Queer as Folk 2*, Vince and his mother
Hazel wander slowly along Canal Street, having left a birthday party for
Nathan being held in the bar Via Fossa. Hazel talks about Stuart's
impending thirtieth birthday, and how his party will probably feature
'elephants and zeppelins'. This phrase – also, incidentally, used by a
character in Davies's *Mine All Mine* – brings to mind circuses and
parades, spectacle and extravagance, and could actually stand in as a
summary of the contents of the first four episodes of *Queer as Folk*.
These instalments, the focus of this chapter, overflow with dramatic
incident: a large number of sex scenes that are messy, noisy and often
funny; a lesbian giving birth to a baby fathered by a gay man; a
character dying from a drug overdose after snorting heroin and his
subsequent funeral; a queer teenager leaping from his closet and running
away from home. And as the narrative pinballs between story strands,
incidents, and set pieces, the cinematography, soundtrack and *mise en
scène* combine to give many sequences a sense of occasion: the style
throughout is frequently glossy and seductive, with a colour and lighting
scheme as brilliant as fireworks. This chapter provides an overview and
critical assessment of a number of *Queer as Folk*'s key elements: its
visual and aural aesthetic, the construction of the three lead characters,
its depictions of sex, cruising and Manchester's gay scene, and its
representations of queer parenting and friendship.

Queer as Folk's characteristic 'blurred background'

23

The visual aesthetic constructed for *Queer as Folk*'s first four episodes by director Charles McDougall (and other members of the creative team) is one of the series' most distinguishing aspects. Nicola Shindler has commented that the inspiration for the look of the show was provided by American drama series such as *L.A. Law* (Fox for NBC, 1986–94) and *Ally McBeal* (David E. Kelley Productions/Fox, 1997–2002): the aim was to set *Queer as Folk* apart from other contemporary British dramas by mimicking an American style.[36] Specific lenses were used to produce a particular aspect of this style: a 'blurred background' of colourful but indistinct lights against which characters would be shot in crisp close-up. Although the rainbow flag – an icon of the gay rights movement, often used by lesbian and gay venues and individuals to proclaim their identity and allegiance – is notably absent in *Queer as Folk*, all the colours of the rainbow are regularly and boldly used in the lighting and set design. At its most striking, this provides certain scenes and images with the gaudy qualities of pop art (a notably queer art movement, according to some academics).[37] The first episode of the series, for instance, contains direct-to-camera monologues from Vince, Stuart and Nathan (a narrative device which does not appear in any other episode), in which each character is framed against a different bright swathe of a single colour. When Stuart picks up Nathan on Canal Street in the same episode, the buildings in the background are illuminated in pale orange and lime green. And in the third episode, in a scene set in the nightclub Babylon, the camera pans over a row of toilet cubicles, each lit a different colour, before it comes to rest above Vince and Stuart. These shots could be compared to the hyperrealistic set designs used by New Queer Cinema film-maker Gregg Araki in his films *The Doom Generation* (1995) and *Nowhere* (1997), in which narrative realism is complicated or challenged by a meticulous – and sometimes distracting – sense of design.

The visual configuration of these episodes is accompanied by a distinctive use of music that persists throughout the run of the series. This soundtrack is composed of three specific elements: Britpop songs; pop, dance and disco tracks; and Murray Gold's score. The Britpop tracks – which include Pulp's 'Common People' and Suede's 'Beautiful Ones' – historically situate *Queer as Folk* in a mid-to-late-90s milieu, but also link the series to the flush of optimism Britain experienced under a recently appointed New Labour government after seventeen years of Tory rule. Countering stereotypes, the use of these guitar-based songs also reveals that some gay men may listen to types of music other than disco or torch songs. The pop and dance tracks range from Blondie's 'One Way or Another' to Kylie Minogue's 'Better the Devil You Know', and from the club remix of Everything but the Girl's 'I Didn't Know I Was Looking for Love' to Urban Cookie Collective's 'The Key the Secret'. A decision was made by the production team not to use the harder-edged dance music that might be found in gay clubs across the UK; utilising more recognisable tracks would make the queer world depicted in *Queer as Folk* accessible to a wider audience. Also notably absent is any 'difficult' or 'threatening' queercore music: Sister

Pop art stylings in *Queer as Folk*

Hyperrealistic set design in Gregg Araki's *Nowhere*

George's tracks sampling serial killer Aileen Wuornos, for instance, or even Pansy Division's 'Dick of Death' or 'Fuck Buddy'. The combination of Britpop, pop and softer dance music in *Queer as Folk* actually gives the series a 'Poptastic' aural aesthetic. Poptastic is a club night originally established in 1996 that has offshoots in several UK cities, including Manchester, Leeds and Nottingham. Out on their first date in episode five, Vince tells Cameron that Poptastic is one of the venues he frequently visits. I was a regular attendee at the Leeds event for several years: like *Queer as Folk* itself, the club was as popular with straight girls as gay boys.

Complementing the Britpop, pop and dance tracks is Murray Gold's score. Throughout his career providing theme tunes and incidental music for television programmes, Gold has regularly worked with Red Productions and Russell T. Davies: he has scored, among other series, *Clocking Off*, *The Second Coming*, *Mine All Mine* and the re-launched *Doctor Who*. His scores tend to be light, melodic and upbeat, signifying 'fun and japes'. Gold's music sometimes operates as part of a drama's specific political project: that is, it works alongside what is depicted to overthrow audience prejudices and assumptions. Briefly summarised, *Queer as Folk* is a story about unrequited love between homosexuals, *Shameless* is a council estate drama about an extended family with a (usually errant) wretchedly alcoholic father, and *Mine All Mine* is a tale about land-ownership set in Swansea. All three might sound dull, worthy and potentially miserable. But the opening credits of each series, all scored by Gold, bounce along swiftly, setting the tone for what is to come. With *Queer as Folk*, for instance, the score begins, briefly, with voices (possibly synthesised) singing in harmony, over which a guitar then starts a jaunty rhythm – a rhythm somewhat reminiscent of the main guitar line in George Michael's song 'Faith'. Marimba join to play the main melodic line, a cheerful rising-and-falling tune, which is accentuated by a number of short synthetic 'whoops'; both swiftly disappear, leaving just the brisk guitar strums. This music accompanies images of swimming lights, blurred and indistinct, under an orange-red filter. The shifting lights may depict a distanced view of Manchester, or they could be the hazy spots of a club's dancefloor – or perhaps, as Antony Cotton has suggested, they are supposed to be sperm seen under a microscope.[38] These credits immediately distance *Queer as Folk* from previous 'gay dramas' on television: this, audiences are reassured, will not be a depressing tale about repressed and unhappy homosexuals.

26

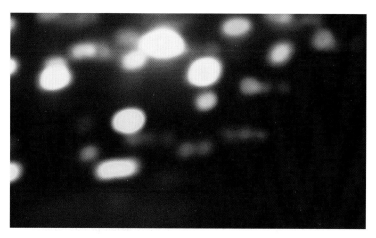

The blurred lights of the intro credits

Stuart's apartment

Although the visual and aural aesthetic established by *Queer as Folk* is distinctive, it has precedents. In particular, it resembles the beguiling sights and sounds of advertising. The bold (and sometimes rather unreal) use of strong colours, the swift edits and dynamic camerawork combine with the soundtrack to produce sequences of seductive moments whose textures echo those of adverts. The lives of these gay characters, this aesthetic implies, are consumerist, their acquisitive sexual practices ('so you wank him off in a doorway and move on', says Vince in the first episode) directly related to their persistent consumption of drugs and drink, and the array of material goods with which they surround themselves. Stuart's loft apartment, in particular, is indicative of this advertising aesthetic. The location is open plan, sizeable, opulent; according to the script, it is 'gorgeous, design straight out of *Wallpaper*'.[39] The space – in reality, a warehouse that was formerly part of the nightclub Sankey's Soap, which closed down in 1998 – reveals Stuart's income bracket, as well as suggesting, in its tidiness, that he doesn't spend too much time there (or that he hires effective cleaners). Large cream sofas are complemented by varnished wooden floors, the beams of the sloping roof, exposed brickwork and, providing a bit of character, a working and stocked snack dispenser machine. There is a significant amount of ambient lighting, including a coloured panel on one wall illuminated either a bold blue (for sequences that take place at night) or yellow (those set during the day). Parts of Canal Street, the epicentre of Manchester's gay scene, are also shot in a similarly alluring manner: the cobbled street itself is adorned with fairy lights and fire torches.

The advertising aesthetic also includes *Queer as Folk*'s music. For example, as in adverts, songs are often used in the programme in literal ways. When Stuart and Nathan first cruise each other on Canal Street in episode one, Indigo's 'Haven't You Heard', which has a pulse like a heartbeat, accompanies the slowed-down images; its lyrics, 'I've been looking for you', seem to directly refer to the seduction depicted. The morning after their first sex together, Stuart and Nathan are met by Vince, who is driving Stuart's jeep: Pulp's 'Something Changed' plays, signifying a shift in the relationship between Vince and Stuart caused by Nathan. And in *Queer as Folk 2*, when Vince turns up at Nathan's sixteenth birthday party having run away from Stuart and his plan to blow up a car, Geri Halliwell's 'Mi Chico Latino' plays. 'Take me back to my sweet la vida', she sings, seemingly a direct comment on Vince's frame of mind, his yearning for the evening's events not to have happened. These uses of music are not that distant from, for instance, discount superstore Argos scoring their colourful adverts with Status Quo's song 'Whatever You Want' ('you pay your money, you take your choice, whatever you need ...').

Queer as Folk's colourful, poppy aesthetic needs to be contextualised in relation to a 1990s cultural shift which attempted to make queer life seem sexy and attractive. Recognising that many lesbians and gay men often have no dependants and thus have greater disposable incomes (however limited), during this decade corporations and advertisers started to appeal to and capitalise on the lucrative 'pink pound'. In order to do so, however, and shake off the pejorative stigma historically associated with queer sexualities and behaviours, a 'mainstreamed' lesbian/gay culture had to be constituted and promulgated: the model disseminated was of a mainly white, healthy, urban and wealthy (or aspirationally so) demographic. The 1990s witnessed the appearance on British newsstands of a number of lesbian and gay lifestyle publications – *Diva*, *Phase*, *Attitude* – targeted at this market. The magazines pitched music and movies (niche or otherwise), holidays and travel, fashion and styling products to their readers; companies advertised a host of consumer goods and services within their pages, from jewellery to literature, from counselling to hair removal. Some sex stores such as Prowler and Clone Zone rebranded and restyled themselves as book and clothing boutiques. The drive broke through to other (more diffuse) media arenas: musician kd lang appeared on the front of *Vanity Fair* being shaved by Cindy Crawford; films such as the Wachowski brothers' *Bound* (1996) featured attractive and empathetic lead characters who weren't straight; television personalities such as Julian Clary, Graham Norton and Lily Savage popularised a saucy, open brand of queerness that appealed beyond a niche gay audience. This 'mainstreamed' queerness evidently had its limits: there was little or no place for the rural, working class or non-white in its representational schemas; people with AIDS, older and disabled queers, and those members of queer subcultural groups (bears, for instance: that is, gay men with facial hair and hairy bodies, who may be heavy-set) were ignored.[40] Thus the trade-off for making images of lesbian and gay people more widespread, and hence accessible (and acceptable) to a wider audience, was to delimit the range of representations available. The politics of this mainstream shift were markedly antagonistic to those of many queer activists: as noted in the introduction, the 'queer' movement was (and still is) concerned with forging coalitions and connections between groups and individuals situated outside of the heteronormative – across boundaries of class, gender, race, and so on.

Queer as Folk occupied a complex position in relation to the cultural mainstreaming of homosexuality in the 1990s. Although its three lead characters were all young white men, their lives centred to a significant extent on the consumerist pleasures of drink, drugs and dancing, their extended social network (as we will see shortly) was more diverse and complicated. Further, the series may have appealed to an audience beyond a core demographic of gay men, but it remained closely focused throughout on the contours of its main characters' queer lives, and incorporated culturally specific references and allusions (such as Vince's penchant for the porn company Cadinot) that only some gay men may have picked up on. And the 'advertising' aesthetic – which was not used consistently throughout Queer as Folk, as many sequences were shot in a more pedestrian or 'realistic' manner – may have made queerness 'sexy', but it also, in doing so, offered a counter to earlier, more bleak and depressing, depictions of homosexuality in television drama. In this sense, the series' bold colour scheme and upbeat score can be interpreted as political in their own right – and, arguably, connected to a longer history of queer cultural output which has favoured (or even delighted in) a brash, gaudy register, from George Cukor's Hollywood melodramas to the music of Rufus Wainwright.

However, the combination of Queer as Folk's poppy visual and aural aesthetic with its depictions of excess and hedonism caused some critics to berate the series for its shallowness. In the Guardian, Sam Wollaston described the series as 'slick and snazzy but rather lacking analysis'.[41] Michael Collins in the Observer called the programme 'the Millennium Dome of homosexuality': 'like the dome', he said, *Queer as Folk* 'looked spectacular, had lots of rides, yet was thin on content'.[42] And yet these judgments are rather unfair. Both the audiovisual design and the content of *Queer as Folk* were detailed, multifaceted and complicated, as this book hopes to show. And although some of its characters revelled in socialising and the pleasures afforded from a disposable income in a capitalist economy (Stuart's flashy jeep is a crucial marker here), this lifestyle was also opened up to criticism. In episode three, one of Vince and Stuart's pals, Phil, picks up a guy called Harvey who offers him drugs: after a snort of heroin, Phil collapses and dies. This death is a narrative shock, the killing off of a significant character, not unlike the death of Helen Flynn (Lisa Faulkner) two episodes into the first season of *Spooks* (BBC, 2002–). At Phil's wake in episode four, his mother confronts Vince about her son's death. Vince tells her that it had nothing to do with being gay; she retorts 'Hasn't it? At thirty-five? *Philip?* He'd find himself at thirty-five taking heroin with a casual *fuck* if he was *straight?*' Her criticisms – of gay male promiscuity, risk-taking and casual drug use – shake Vince, as they contain the suggestion that he, as part of a scene that fosters and supports particular behaviours and attitudes, is to some degree responsible for Phil's death. Later in the same episode, Vince, still upset, lambasts the repetitive and compulsive behaviours of some gay men: 'We're getting older but there's nothing to stop us, so we don't. We never bloody stop.' In *Queer as Folk 2*, even Stuart eventually recognises and disparages the claustrophobic nature of the Manchester scene: 'my world is so bloody huge', he says, hanging over a nightclub balcony.

Condemning *Queer as Folk* for being 'thin on content' also ignores the fact that many of the series' characters develop considerable depth, and operate as empathetic figures. In relation to this concern, opening the first episode with a direct-to-camera speech from Vince was a strategic decision. After the brief credits, there is a cut to our first view of him, on his own, monologue mid-flow, framed in medium close-up in a blue polo shirt against a bright yellow backdrop. He talks to the camera as if it were one of his friends, the warmth of his casual speech

Vince talking to the camera in episode one

32   augmented by the primary colours. The particular cadences and content
of gay male speech – irony, flippancy, overt sexual comment, obtuse
cultural reference points – are combined with a Manchester accent and
northern colloquialisms. Vince is set up as the easiest character to
identify with, positioned as an 'average guy' who works in middle
management in a supermarket called Harlo's. He is the most sensible of
the three lead characters – Vince regularly looks after the jeep and baby
Alfred for Stuart, and he is the one who realises Hazel has to take in
Nathan as a lodger, in case the teenager's threats about running away to
London lead to harm. He has a sharp sense of humour and an open,
warm face. 'Vince has the look of someone who *needs* loving', wrote
Duncan Marr, 'which is terribly persuasive if you're wondering which of
the characters you might like to fall in love with'.[43] Vince adores his
Mum, and supports her financially with his presumably fairly average
earnings. But he is also rather pitiable: not only is he closeted at work,
but he is a pop-culture geek, particularly fond of *Doctor Who* (a pair of
blue boxer shorts decorated with a Dalek motif were made for his

character by the costume team, but never used). Vince makes self-deprecating gags about his love life and physical appearance ('He takes his kit off, Marky Mark, I take mine off, Norman Wisdom'); this is coupled to his unconsummated relationship with Stuart, which serves as a powerful emotive undertow to the interactions between the two. Near the end of the second episode, Vince unearths a photograph of Barry Sheene that he and Stuart once had an (interrupted) sexual encounter over as teenagers: Vince still has the picture stored away in a box at his mother's house. The photo operates as his Rosebud, signifying a lost and idealised moment of happiness he can never again attain. (This comparison with *Citizen Kane* [1941] can be sustained: in a scene set in Babylon in episode three, Vince delivers a short speech about attractive men spotted across a crowded club that echoes a similar – heterosexual – monologue in Orson Welles's film). And yet Vince is also a coward and a liar: at several points in *Queer as Folk* and its sequel, he makes up pathetic excuses to scarper from unsavoury situations. Only twice does he significantly break from his position of sensible stability: at the end of episode four, when he walks out of Hazel's house and runs away (he is back in the supermarket by the start of the next instalment); and at the end of the sequel, when he leaves Manchester with Stuart for Arizona.

33

Stuart, in contrast, is the id to Vince's ego. (The role, incidentally, was initially offered to Christopher Eccleston, who turned it down.) One of the significant mental leaps that needs to be made by audiences of *Queer as Folk* lies in believing that Stuart and Vince would still be friends after fifteen years. Stuart's job, home and character are markedly different to Vince's: he is fickle, unpredictable, quicksilver. Often quiet and reticent, Stuart rarely cracks jokes or laughs, although he does smirk and giggle. And yet he is also cocky and brash, sexually predatory and, unlike Vince, usually seems to have great sex. 'I want to die shagging', he says in episode four, and in a line cut from the sequel Alexander refers to Stuart as 'Erogenous Jones'. *Queer as Folk* does not suggest that the sex Stuart has is radical in itself (this argument about queer sexual activity has been made by, for instance, Jean Genet and Charley Shiveley).[44] But in relation to the ongoing widespread assumption of an association between gay men and HIV/AIDS, depicting Stuart as unapologetically sexually promiscuous was a daring strategy. Lacking a sense of caution, Stuart indulges in immediate actions and pleasures; when surrounded by his own mess in episode one, he bleats 'Why doesn't anyone stop me? It's not my fault', as though he is not responsible and requires taming and controlling. Stuart is frequently positioned as the lead character in the series, a figure of fascination who sometimes stares back at the camera, inviting a response. Around 10 per cent of *Queer as Folk*'s costume budget was spent on outfitting Aidan Gillen, dressing him as a strutting peacock. As costume designer Pam Tait has pointed out:

> He [Gillen] wanted a sort of sense of sheen about the guy, which was completely fine with me because of course he is all surface. I mean, there's a lot beneath, but ... he's the alpha gay, glittering. He had a Paul Smith suit ... that was very fine black with a print lining. There was another Jigsaw suit, some trousers ... Some composition-soled loafers, that were very easy, because I thought he should pad ... Lots of shirts and big ties. It was just when Gucci had done that thing of having dark shirts and dark ties, and again with a slight sheen ... So here's the kind of taste of him: flimsy, light and shiny, and deadly. But by I think episode four, I said, 'Well, I'm just dressing you as Satan now' – I didn't say that to him – but we just put him in red and black, because he really suits dark red, and of course that's a real pull on screen, and so he was either red and black, or black and red.

In the first episodes of *Queer as Folk*, Stuart's outfits serve as a constituent element of the 'elephants and zeppelins' aesthetic: in episode one, he wears a striking textured yellow jumper to attend the hospital where his son Alfred has just been born; later in the same instalment, he sports a bold blue suit with a red tie fastened in a fat knot, the clash of colours both stylish and distinctive. His later styling as Satan is subtly reflected in Alfred's costuming: in episode five, for instance, the infant wears a red hat with two pronged horns. Russell T. Davies suggested in an interview in *Gay Times* in 2000 that 'What I keep in mind a lot of the time when I'm writing [*Queer as Folk*] is that we are all Vince, we can be Stuart, we were all Nathan.'[45] Stuart, then, is a complex figure: a character whose lifestyle might be enviable to some audience members but repellent to others, who may act as a figure of fantasy, but whose mercurial personality might hamper or impede audience empathy.

Stuart as Satan

35

Alfred as the spawn of Satan

From a political perspective, the differences between Stuart and Vince could perhaps be seen to position them as analogous representatives of the two most visible gay/queer activist and lobbying groups in the UK, OutRage! and Stonewall, both of which were formed in the late 1980s. Vince, who enjoys the pleasures of the gay scene but would prefer not to disturb the status quo, stands for the assimilationist aims of Stonewall. In contrast, disruptive Stuart, who embodies the aspects of queer existence most threatening to conservative attitudes – multiple sexual partners, often at the same time; parenting a child with two lesbians; shaping provocative media representations of partially clothed male bodies through his job (a point of connection between Stuart and Russell T. Davies, perhaps) – stands for the more radical aims of OutRage!. In the sequel, this discrepancy becomes more pronounced, and needs to be assuaged in order for satisfactory narrative resolution.

Nathan, in contrast to the two older men, is a teenager in formation. He embarrasses himself – he calls Vince's mother 'a mong' in episode two, not knowing who she is – and has yet to learn appropriate codes of conduct among gay men. He steals phrases and ideas from more mature characters: in episode five, he pilfers both Stuart's line 'You can see me now', and Dazz's poster slogan about the 'fascist heterosexual orthodoxy'. Both Nathan and his pal Donna reveal a tendency to chunter away. When first taken back to Stuart's flat in episode one, Nathan burbles on about cooking, about takeaways, about experiencing anaphylactic shock. Charlie Hunnam's delivery effectively captures the toe-curling awkwardness of teenagers out of their depth but desperate to fit in, and the dialogue reveals Davies's ability to write believable adolescent characters, presumably honed while working in children's drama. As Hazel puts it, Nathan 'explodes' from the closet: he gets caught up in his own drama, his inflated egotism encapsulated in his exclamations 'I'm *doing* it! I'm really doing it' (that is, having sex, unlike many of his peers), and 'I'm Mozart! I'm fucking Mozart!' (in other words, breaking new ground at a young age). Although Nathan has his first queer sexual experiences with Stuart, he ends up living at Vince's mother's house: the concern for audiences in relation to his broader narrative arc is whether Nathan will become more like Stuart or Vince.

Here it is worth noting that the first few scenes of *Queer as Folk*, as originally scripted and shot, were notably different to what was screened as the final edit. The first episode of the series was initially intended to begin with Nathan getting off a bus and walking along Canal Street, witnessing some of the exciting and alarming spectacle of the place. In other words, Nathan was initially intended to serve as the audience's proxy, introducing them to Manchester's queer scene. This narrative role does not entirely vanish from the series. In episode three, for instance, Nathan warns Donna before they enter Babylon for the first time, 'If there's blokes kissing, right, don't stare at them, and if you see men who look like women don't stare at them either ...'. This sentence seems like a comment to intrepid audience members at home, too, a warning of how to behave in unfamiliar territory: Donna, as a straight girl, might be seen as the stand-in for any heterosexual women (and others) watching at home who have never been to a gay club before. But the filmed scenes of Nathan's first venture onto Canal Street in episode one, once complete, were judged to be rather bleak. As Davies has noted:

> It was assembled in the edit exactly as written, and it was like a thriller. You expected Stuart to take Nathan home and murder him, like an episode of *Cracker*. [. . .] So, we had a big problem, the opening ten minutes of ep.1 were scary and tense. Fortunately, we were still filming, so I was able to go away and write a completely new piece-to-camera for Vince. He becomes your narrator, someone safe, relaxed, smiling, leading you into that world.[46]

This comment certainly explains why the narrative initially introduces Vince, Phil and Stuart, and then seems to loop chronologically backwards, in a fairly smooth temporal ellipsis, to the arrival of Nathan on Canal Street. It also highlights a crucial element of the final edit: that Vince replaces Nathan as the audience's first narrative point of contact, setting him up as an empathetic figure and a friendly interlocutor.

37

Stuart doesn't murder Nathan, but he does have sex with him. These scenes of sexual intimacy generated significant amounts of attention and discussion. On the day after the first instalment of *Queer as Folk* was broadcast, Channel 4 received 321 telephone calls about the show: 136 complaints, and 185 messages of praise and support.[47] (The calls, both for and against, continued throughout the series' run.) Criticisms came from various quarters of the press. Linda Lee-Potter, the *Daily Mail* journalist, claimed that *Queer as Folk* was 'virtually a live sex show, which is indefensible'; she also argued that the programme was 'exploiting young gay men in order to give cheap thrills to inadequate, sad viewers'.[48] Kevin Myers, in the *Sunday Telegraph*, stated that

> *Queer as Folk* was a self-indulgent, self-justifying delectation of the sodomisation of under-age boys. The events portrayed were criminal events, and even though the boy was shown as a 'consenting' partner, he was violated by an adult male who knew that he was just 15. Nor was there any admission that something monstrous was going on. Quite the reverse; buggery was seen as liberation ...[49]

And in *Gay Times*, Terry Sanderson, despite largely praising the series, added

> I did think that the sex scenes were needlessly provocative and extended to the point where they were bound to cause controversy. They went on for maybe fifteen seconds too long for any convincing claim that they weren't meant to get Middle England foaming at the mouth. The man and his boyfriend had already discussed rimming, so did we really have to see tongue on bottom to get the idea? That's the stuff of porn, not serious drama; but Channel 4 needs the ratings ...[50]

The sex sequences in episode one of *Queer as Folk*, the 'tongue on bottom' and the sodomy, were scandalous not only because they depicted explicit queer carnal relations on the small screen, but because

38

they featured an adult man having (illegal) sex with a minor. Nathan and Stuart's coupling directly challenged the arbitrary nature of the age of consent, as well as long-held assumptions regarding the sexual identities and behaviours of teenagers. In this regard, it is useful to compare Nathan with other queer teenagers on the small screen: Jack in *Dawson's Creek* (Outerbank Entertainment/Columbia Tristar for WB, 1998–2003), Willow and Tara in *Buffy the Vampire Slayer* (Mutant Enemy/Kuzui/Sandollar for Fox, 1997–2003), Alex in *As If* (Carnival Films for Channel 4, 2001–4). Although all of these other characters developed same-sex relationships, their containment within the genre form of 'youth television' restricted the explicit content depicted. Indeed, Nathan's graphically portrayed sexual activities have more in common with those of teenagers in particular New Queer Cinema titles, such as Gregg Araki's *Totally F***ed Up* (1993). Connections can also be made with the British film *Beautiful Thing* (1996), adapted for the screen by Jonathan Harvey from his own play: Jamie (Glen Berry), like Nathan, has a strong and supportive mother, and a black girl as a close ally. Though less sexually explicit than *Queer as Folk*, MacDonald's film also tackled the thorny issue of teenage homosexuality. In addition to *Queer as Folk*'s depiction of a sexually aware queer teenager, the series' representations of anal sex and rimming on television, even on a minority channel after the watershed, confronted restrictions regarding 'appropriate' material for the medium. Whether the scenes were 'salacious' or 'overly long' is difficult to judge, especially when the number of previous representations of queer sex on television had been so sparse; besides, such evaluations would almost certainly be inflected by complicated personal attitudes towards the depiction of sexual behaviour in screen fictions.

39

The sex between Nathan and Stuart in episode one is shot in a manner in keeping with the rest of the episode: the colour and lighting use is seductive, tan skin against white sheets. Although there is no sign of an erect penis (one taboo too far for Channel 4, perhaps, as such an image would be illegal) it is evident that the actors are fully naked. Close-ups are intercut with wider shots that provide more access to the

Sex mid-shot, episode one

The audience being sodomised by Stuart

scene: this stands in notable contrast to, for instance, the short sex scenes between men in the TV adaptation of David Leavitt's book *The Lost Language of Cranes* (WNET/BBC, 1991), which are rather dark and murky, and which tend to cut before the action starts, or only focus in on faces. When Nathan ejaculates, Stuart has to shake the matter off his hand: there is no shying away from the mess produced. Perhaps most provocatively, one shot positions the audience with Nathan, on his back, looking up into Stuart's sweaty and leering face. For a few brief moments, it is the audience being sodomised. Russell T. Davies has pointed out that the Stuart/Nathan sex sequences were included for strategic narrative reasons:

> With the sex scenes in episode one it's story, it's as simple as that. I mean, it's a boy getting his mind fucked as he's buggered. [. . .] And it's fascinating that verbally in the same episode, there's a monologue to camera from Stuart where he describes having sex with a gym teacher when he was twelve. No one ever mentions that – there's no fuss about that. And that's willing consensual sex with a twelve-year-old who goes into his teacher's shower. But you don't see a naked arse in that – so therefore you don't panic. [. . .] The most important thing in that first sex scene is the premature ejaculation. Nathan cums too soon and that affects the entire ten episodes – he always thinks he's let that man down. And in thinking that, he also – complicatedly – falls in love with him and always has to make something up to him.[51]

Certainly, the sex scenes in *Queer as Folk* do seem to be present either in order to develop the story, or to act as comedic interludes (and some operate as both). Only one scene in episode three, in which Stuart films his involvement in a threesome and then enjoys watching it back with the other men, does not seem to further the narrative – although it contributes to the audience's understanding of Stuart as sexually voracious. (The Broadcasting Standards Commission stated that this depiction of troilism exceeded the boundaries of what is acceptable on television.) It is notable that the amount of sexual activity in *Queer as Folk* diminishes across the episodes: there is very little in the second half of the series, and almost none in the sequel. The overt sexual content of *Queer as Folk* provides a link between the series and *Sex and the City* – indeed, their appearance on British television at almost the same time seems serendipitous. Not only did both programmes appeal to both straight women and gay men, but both challenged televisual regimes regarding depictions of sexual behaviour and sexual language. Almost all of the main characters in the two series had frequent, graphically depicted sex; and almost all talked honestly and directly about sex in ways never previously shown on television. These connections between the series clearly account for the weekly scheduling of the programmes together as a Saturday-night double bill during *Queer as Folk*'s run.

Scenes of brazen sexuality also feature in the opening minutes of episode two of *Queer as Folk*, which presents a skilfully choreographed montage of Vince, Stuart and Nathan cruising the men around them, the stares and movements of the men intercut and set to the track 'Sexy Boy' by Air (another rather literal use of music). Nathan confidently swaggers down the corridors at school, turning to walk backwards at one point so that he can take in the pleasurable sight of a fellow schoolboy's arse. Vince, at work at Harlo's, wanders the aisles with pen and clipboard; the guy he cruises turns out to be shopping with his boyfriend. Vince's colleague Marcie makes a limp-wristed gesture behind the gay couple's back, at which closeted Vince laughs – and is caught doing so by the couple. Stuart, meanwhile, eyes up a married client arriving at the PR firm he works for. Opportunistically pinning on a metal AIDS ribbon – he uses it to show his availability to other men, not to demonstrate any kind of compassion or charity – Stuart sits opposite the client for the work presentation and blatantly stares at him.

This sustained sequence is one of the most radical in *Queer as Folk*, in terms of the challenge it presents to dominant regimes of representation. It explicitly invites viewers to use their eyes in ways comparable to the three lead gay male characters, providing access to an overtly sexualised queer gaze. That is, it explicitly exposes the mechanics of cruising – knowing how and when to sneak a glance, the pleasures taken in the illicit ogle, the discomfort or arousal that a lengthy and brazen stare by one man at another can provoke – and invites viewers to participate. The intercutting highlights that Stuart, Vince and Nathan are all looking at other men in ways similar to each

Nathan cruising

Stuart cruising

Vince cruising

other; with them, the viewer is invited to also 'cruise' the public locations depicted, and to objectify the men being looked at. Writing about this sequence in *Queer as Folk*, Glen Creeber has noted that:

> This 'gay gaze' unsettles the very apparatus upon which looking has tended to be constructed in conventional heterosexual discourse, producing another level of meaning that inherently undermines traditional notions of who should be looked at and by whom. As a result, the viewer is asked to view the world from a radically different point of view, one that disturbs and re-constructs the very means by which television has traditionally viewed and portrayed homosexuality in the past.[52]

This isn't the only moment in *Queer as Folk* when cruising dynamics are in operation, merely the most conspicuous. In other episodes, shots of the main characters are sometimes purposefully intercut with their sexualised points of view, so that we are also enabled to scan their location (bar, club, street) for erotic pleasure and potential: in sequences in episode three and in the second episode of *Queer as Folk 2*, for instance, lead characters lean over a nightclub's balcony, scanning the dancefloor for new meat, passing catty comment ('The sad twat, he's wearing cheesecloth. Is cheesecloth back?') and identifying sexual opportunity.

Is it possible that there are connections between the activities of cruising and watching television? R. Bruce Brassell, in an article on Andy Warhol's 1965 film *My Hustler*, has suggested that the movie constructs a spectatorial regime of 'glancing practices [which] position spectators as part of [a] community of gay men'. With glancing, 'The viewing experience is selective, whether that be where we focus on the screen or how attentive we are to the sound track.'[53] Since the publication of Laura Mulvey's well-known 1975 essay 'Visual Pleasure and Narrative Cinema', film theory has discussed movie spectatorship in relation to the 'gaze'; in contrast, John Ellis has posited that television viewing is characterised by 'glancing'.[54] Bringing Brassell and Ellis's arguments together suggests that prevalent modes of consuming television – that is, distracted 'glancing' – may have affiliations with cruising, in ways that *Queer as Folk* both taps into and reveals.

Key moments of cruising in *Queer as Folk* occur in gay bars and clubs; long sections of the first four episodes of the series are spent in such venues. It is worth noting that the depiction of gay pubs and nightclubs in *Queer as Folk* is markedly different to most previous representations in British television and cinema. The pubs and clubs in Ron Peck's film *Nighthawks* (1978) and in *The Lost Language of Cranes*, for instance, are dimly lit, rather bleak spaces; they are places in which solitary drinkers dance and cruise to brutal industrial music, and socialisation is limited. This is in stark contrast to the messy explosion of people, noise, light and décor that fills the queer venues depicted throughout *Queer as Folk*. The first we are allowed inside is the New Union, in episode two. Brash splashes of colour are produced by a lighting rig attached to the low ceiling in the small but well-populated space; they illuminate lesbians and gay men dancing and drinking, a varied clientele which includes clones in peaked caps and a number of hefty men in drag. Via Fossa, a second bar, is larger and busier, a little more upmarket, with exposed brickwork and tables to sit around. The music in both venues is upbeat and poppy: Kylie Minogue, Blondie. Gub Neal and Catriona MacKenzie at Channel 4 wanted the series to feature trendier bars of the chrome-and-pine variety, but Shindler and Davies insisted on using more standard, somewhat shabby pub venues for their warmth and familiarity to a broader range of audiences.

The nightclub Babylon – its name evoking luxury, corruption, exile – is depicted as a particularly colourful and seductive environment, a space of marvellous possibility. The first visit to the venue occurs in episode three. This scene, like similar ones in the films *Trainspotting* (1996) and *Human Traffic* (1999), attempts to distil the social, affective, erotic and narcotic pleasures of clubbing into several minutes of screen time. As Nathan and Donna enter and descend into the club, there is a reprise of the dance track – Indigo's 'Haven't You Heard' – that accompanied Stuart and Nathan first cruising each other in episode one, the reappearance of the song suggesting that this sequence is also of

The bar in *Nighthawks*

The New Union

Babylon

momentous significance for Nathan. Fairy lights are wound around the handrails of the stairs, at the bottom of which there are large Egyptian figurines. Tall transparent plastic tubes are filled with bubbling liquid and lit orange, blue and green. There are metallic drapes hanging from the ceiling, a requisite disco ball, neon strips in pink and blue, men and women dancing on podiums and a small stage, a crowded dancefloor, balconies handy for people-watching, and lights relentlessly strafing the space. Babylon's heterodox set design identifies the club as a site in which 'anything goes'.

All of these locations are depicted as friendly, safe spaces in which carefree hedonism is encouraged. The patrons in some of the venues, especially the New Union, are varied in age and gender, contributing to a model of the gay scene as welcoming, as a community focus, as accepting of diversity. (The focus on busy bright spaces in *Queer as Folk* is, of course, a limited depiction of the gay scene: although they might not be venues that Vince and Stuart would visit, there are no leather or fetish bars, no bear clubs, no 'underwear only' theme nights.) The upbeat ambience and gaudy colour schemes of the Canal Street pubs and clubs depicted in the series are contrasted, in episode two, with an average straight bar that Vince visits, after agreeing to join some of his co-workers from Harlo's supermarket for a drink. Vince is on the phone to Stuart as he enters the location:

47

> It's all true. Everything we've ever been told. Oh my God, everything but flock wallpaper. Ohh, and the people! There are people talking in sentences that have no punchline and they don't even care. Can you believe it, they've got toilets in which no one's ever had sex.

The inside of the straight pub is banal: brown panelled walls, sunlight filtered through net curtains, indistinct framed pictures, floral-patterned seating, small chintzy wall lights. Wayne Fontana and the Mindbenders' song 'The Game of Love' plays in the background, its lyrics ('the purpose of a man is to love a woman, the purpose of a woman is to love a man') only adding further to the heterosexuality of the venue.

The straight bar

48   Vince's ironic monologue reveals the marked segregation between the
gay scene and the straight world, a distance that *Queer as Folk* regularly
highlights for comedic or dramatic purposes. Some of the most
memorable sequences in the series centre on queer characters impinging
upon and disrupting 'straight' spaces and events: weddings, funerals,
hospitals, suburban streets, school classrooms. Vince and Stuart drive
Nathan to school at the end of episode one in a vehicle graffitied with
the word 'QUEERS': they zoom up the avenue to the building in a
manner designed to generate attention. When Phil and Vince meet
Alexander at the airport at the start of episode three, he is dressed in a
striking purple suit and bug shades ('Miss Corke's wardrobe by
Kamizole', he says, a line stolen from the end credits of *Neighbours*; the
suit actually cost £20 from Agnès B). And at Phil's funeral in episode
four, the church's morose organ music gives way to Sarah Brightman's
'I Lost My Heart to a Starship Trooper'; Vince, delivering a eulogy,
reads out the lyrics to Ottawan's hit single 'D.I.S.C.O.' as though they
were written by Auden. Such sequences serve to reveal the invisible and

unmarked heterosexuality of such sites and ceremonies; placing noisy queer characters within them unmoors their accepted codes of conduct, momentarily rendering the events and places as perverse.

Queer as Folk also 'queers' other concerns and institutions indelibly associated with heterosexuality: most notably, parenting. Stuart may treat Alfred's birth with some flippancy – 'Most expensive wank I've ever had' – but when his position as the boy's father is challenged by Lance in the second half of the series, he acts ruthlessly. Lisa and Romey were not, of course, the first dyke parents to be depicted on television; to take just one example, Ross's son Ben in Friends is raised in collaboration with his lesbian ex and her partner. (In fact, the jokes at the expense of the lesbians in the US sitcom, with the word 'lesbian' itself seeming to prompt laughter from the studio audience, are not that far removed from the gay male dismissals of the dykes in Queer as Folk.) The innovation of Queer as Folk is to depict the difficulties of queer parenting. In episode two, Stuart is asked to sign a 'Security of Provision' arrangement: 'you could get … ill' says Romey, one of the series' only references to HIV/AIDS. Stuart pretends to be fine with the contract, but is actually livid. ('Fucking bastard cunts!' he yells in his jeep as soon as he leaves their house, an outburst that was criticised by the Broadcasting Standards Commission.) Stuart actually struggles to reconcile his nocturnal behaviours with responsible parenthood. And in order to maintain her position in the lesbian household as a co-parent, Lisa has to act maliciously behind Romey's back, securing Lance's deportation. Although the series does not explicitly debate the politics of same-sex parenting, it provokes reflection: if lesbians and gay men have children together, does this mimic heterosexuality, or challenge it? Is the most radical form of queerness, as Lee Edelman argues, actually that which revels in an antipathy towards offspring, in its own lack of futurity?[55]

49

Stuart's interactions with Lisa and Romey operate as just one strand of the series' interrogations of relationships and alliances between and across specific identity groups. The introduction to Hazel and her house in episode two, for instance, highlights a significant political dimension of *Queer as Folk*: that the bonds that exist between the queer characters and their friends have been forged, and continue to function, irrespective of class status. As already noted, Stuart's apartment is a glossy hyperreal fantasy, the huge space furnished with a selection of designer consumer products. Vince's flat, in contrast, is cluttered and tightly framed – there is never a wide shot of the space, suggesting that it is too small to be filmed in such a way. The first few episodes of *Queer as Folk* expose that Vince was raised by his single mother in a poky house in a working-class terrace. In contrast, later in the series it is shown that Stuart's parents are still married and live in a notably middle-class area. Vince is a middle manager in a supermarket, and when at work tends to be shown surrounded by pedestrian items such as toilet rolls or frozen burgers; Stuart works in a gleaming building as an account director at a PR firm, a Patrick Bateman-like job that revolves around surface appearance, aspiration and status. Both men support their families financially: in episode five, Stuart writes his sister Marie a cheque for £500 without batting an eye; in the first episode of *Queer as Folk 2*, Vince hands his mother £100 to help her out. Stuart also assists Vince with money: a scene cut from episode six reveals that Stuart has always paid for Vince's mobile phone; in episode seven, in addition to buying Vince a splashy gift for his thirtieth birthday, Stuart suggests that the two of them might live together ('We could get a house, I'll pay').

Only midway through *Queer as Folk 2* is the class gap between Vince and Stuart explicitly commented on. When Stuart is becoming violent, exacting retribution by blowing up a car, Vince refuses to get involved, and tells Stuart 'You're on your own': 'There's people relying on me, Mum and that house. I end up paying the mortgage every other month; that lot don't earn tuppence. I can't …'. Stuart, it is suggested, can afford to behave wantonly, even criminally, whereas Vince, supporting dependants from his average salary, cannot. Ultimately, however, the two re-forge their alliance: their bond of friendship, fundamentally tied to their sexual otherness, is more important to *Queer as Folk*'s politics than their different class backgrounds and income brackets. This connection also overcomes national differences: whereas Vince and Hazel are English, Stuart and his family are from Ireland. (Aidan Gillen was born in Dublin; his character was not originally written as Irish, but this was incorporated into the script once he had been cast.) These alliances across fundamental segregations of identity – national boundaries, class differences – are vital to the operations of a broader queer politics which, as noted in the introduction to this book, attempts to surpass schisms of class, race, nationality and gender that have previously existed between lesbians, gay men, bisexuals and members of other groups of sexual dissidents.

This is not to say that these divisions between characters in *Queer as Folk* are all bridged, leading to the depiction of a cohesive and supportive queer community (which would, arguably, produce terribly dull drama). On the contrary, the series contains numerous instances of prejudicial comment and behaviour. Romey and Lisa are usually referred to simply as 'the lesbians'. The gay male characters often crack jokes at their expense, and their appearances in some episodes are minimal: they aren't in episode two, for instance, and only Romey features in episode three, pushing a buggy in the background, without any lines. Nathan's concentration on his own coming-out drama does not allow much room for concern about his friend Donna's life – or, crucially, her experiences as a black teenage girl. Stuart's treatment of his assistant Sandra verges on the misogynistic. And the comments and attitudes expressed by some of the gay and lesbian characters towards non-white individuals – East Asian Lee in episode three, Lance from Ghana in episodes five to eight – are overtly racist. For the audience, this complicates the characters as figures of identification: having forged empathetic relationships, possibly, with Vince and his social circle, viewers then need to work out how to accommodate these individuals' racist comments, such as Vince referring to Lee as 'Fu Manchu'.

Davies has commented at length on these concerns:

Nicola Shindler and I were practically attacked by lesbians in the street because of the lack of lesbianism ... In fact [*Queer as Folk*] doesn't [just]

51

ignore lesbians, it actually takes the piss out of lesbians, which is exactly
what gay men do. I mean, of course, there are plenty of gay men and
lesbians that are friends but actually, culturally, it's very strange that these
men and these women are expected to be part of the same homogeneous
group ... And with gay men there is also a fantastically frightening amount
of misogyny towards women, full stop. I've been accused of misogyny with
this programme, the way [the male characters] talk about the women ...
[but] the way they take the piss out of the lesbians, and the way that Stuart
treats his secretary ... are what gay men are like sometimes. [...] There's
also the racism issue here. We were told off by a lot of people ... that we
didn't do enough to cast enough black actors, and they've got a point ...
That was a mistake of ours in the first four episodes. [Re: Lance plotline]:
It's monstrously racist ... I've had people say to me 'ooh, it was so racist,
that', and you sit there going 'actually, it's deliberately racist'. Because
again, I think gay society is also racist ...[56]

In other words, rather than offering up a model of what a utopian queer
cultural politics would look and sound like, *Queer as Folk* favoured
directly confronting and depicting the sexism, misogyny and racism of
its queer characters, as well as the attitudes towards lesbians held and
expressed by some gay men. As we will see in Chapter 3, the racial
politics of British queer culture reappeared as a significant concern in
Queer as Folk 2.

As this chapter has shown then, despite criticisms of the glossy
advertising-like aesthetic adopted by *Queer as Folk*, both the
audiovisual design and the content of the series were complex and
sophisticated. Significant political arguments and issues were raised
within the series' first four episodes, historical modes of depicting
lesbian/gay characters and venues were challenged, and specific aspects
of queer culture (such as cruising) were depicted in detail and at length.
The programme proposed ways in which heterosexual spaces and
institutions could be queered, and how alliances between queer
individuals might be constructed across, or hindered by, other identity
variables. In keeping with the aims of Russell T. Davies to challenge

positive imagery, *Queer as Folk* did not shy away from making its characters opinionated and prejudiced, occasionally vindictive and self-serving. Although the style of the series altered somewhat in its second half, the political aims of its creators persisted – and new ideas and strategies were added to the mix.

2 Party Rings, Angel Delight, Nappies

Near the beginning of episode five of *Queer as Folk*, Vince is shopping in Harlo's with his staff discount. He's on the phone to Hazel, who orders Weetabix for her new lodger, Nathan. 'I'm not shopping for him!' blurts Vince, exasperated; 'What else does he want – party rings? Angel Delight? Nappies?' These pedestrian domestic items for infants give some indication of the content of the second half of the series. For after four episodes of sex and death, drugs and drink, clubbing and socialising, *Queer as Folk* calms down. The register of the last four instalments is notably quieter: they are more closely focused on the detail of characters and minor incidents, the mundane and everyday, than concerned about dazzling viewers with spectacular cinematography and energetic set pieces. Many scenes involve quiet conversations in domestic spaces or in quotidian locations such as city parks, with these exchanges often shot in tight close-up, or utilising fairly statically staged tableaux. This shift in tone comes in part from the input of the director of episodes five to eight, Sarah Harding, described by Russell T. Davies as 'a very different director [to Charles McDougall] – she's much more intimate actually, and character-led.'[57]

The change of focus is also embodied in the scripts. When Channel 4 first commissioned *Queer as Folk*, one of the stipulations made by the station was that Davies, multitasking as writer and co-producer, should not be responsible for scripting all eight episodes.

Davies and Shindler therefore arranged for another writer to pen episodes five and six, from outlines put together by Davies. These completed scripts, however, delivered late in the day, were judged to be of an unsuitable quality. This meant that, at the proverbial eleventh hour, Davies had to step in and swiftly produce two additional scripts, each of which he wrote in about three days. The writer of the abandoned episodes five and six – the scripts, Craig Kelly recalls, featured a scene in which Vince got covered in ice-cream[58] – has never been named, for reasons of discretion and professional propriety.

Davies dislikes these instalments; he describes part six, in particular, as a 'badly written episode' in which 'nothing really happens'.[59] He acknowledges that the division of writing labour on the series – which ultimately did not work – affected the narrative form and structure of the series as a whole:

> It divorced the second half of the series of the need for plot. Cos not much happens – all you get in the next few episodes is just different characteristics of Stuart, Vince and Nathan in different combinations. There's no great big story driving it, because I refused to give any story to the new writer … cos I refused to relinquish the story. And as a result, it now becomes *purely* a character piece.[60]

Davies's critique of his own work is somewhat disingenuous, as episodes five and six actually contain a significant number of narrative events, including the beginning of Vince's relationship with Cameron, Stuart's confrontation with Nathan's father, Roy Maloney, and the introduction of Lance, Romey's friend from Ghana whom she almost marries. All three of these narrative threads lead to dramatic concluding scenes in episode eight. Parts five and six also contain their fair share of memorable scenes and sharp gags, and some smart political commentary.

And yet there are clear tell-tale signs that episodes five and six were written in a hurry. The dramatic and emotional cliffhanger ending of episode four, with Vince running off into the sunset, is all but

55

forgotten, only acknowledged by one line of dialogue in episode five –
Stuart's 'So we're talking now?', when Vince phones him for a crisis
conference about Cameron. Similarly, the narrative transition from
episode six to seven is established only by a brief conversation between
Stuart and Cameron near the end of episode six, in which Stuart asks
what they're going to do for Vince's birthday. Episode six was actually
too short when first edited, and additional material had to be written on
the hoof, including a flimsy exchange between Cameron and Hazel
about teabags. In this regard, it is interesting to compare this hastily
produced sequence with the first episode, which also contains scenes
written at the last minute. The bells and whistles of episode one – its
snappy pace, sex and crane shots – allow viewers to overlook its rather
odd structure. In contrast, by episode six the characters have become
familiar to the audience, and thus can get away with having rather
pedestrian conversations.

   Vince's relationship with Cameron is one of the most
significant narrative threads in the second half of the series. Australian
Cameron – familiar to some viewers as Shane Ramsay from the soap
Neighbours (Grundy/Network Ten, 1985–) – was briefly introduced in

Cameron

episode four at Phil's wake. Aside from a pithy crack from Alexander in episode six, 'Down Under, didgeridoos, mammals with pouches – loads of material, fab', little is made of Cameron's nationality. He pursues Vince, and takes him out for dinner to a trendy restaurant: 'Oh my God, I'm here, I'm going in', says Vince on his mobile to Stuart, recalling his expedition to the straight pub in episode two, and revealing how alien this location is in relation to his usual experience. Cameron offers up a model of an alternative form of gay life. He is 'non-scene', which Vince finds difficult to comprehend, and a little older at thirty-six. He isn't camp or bitchy, and considering Australia's reputation for producing camp cultural output – Kylie Minogue, Dame Edna Everage, *Prisoner Cell Block H* (Grundy/Network Ten, 1979–86), *Kath and Kim* (ABC, 2002–) – this seems like a strategic decision on the behalf of the production team to undermine expectations. Cameron slowly gives in to Vince's bar-and-club lifestyle, but this brings him into an antagonistic power battle with Stuart for Vince's affections. (In fact, it might be that Vince only finds Cameron attractive after Stuart hits on the older man at the end of episode five.) There are marked confrontations between Stuart and Cameron in episode six. Cameron criticises Stuart for his part in provoking an altercation between Nathan and his father: 'So long as you've got a good story for the pub you're happy.' More significantly, after watching Vince and Stuart dance and take ecstasy together on the dancefloor at Babylon (Phil's death evidently had no lasting impact on their casual drug consumption), Cameron faces up to Stuart in a quieter, rather opulent bar. Shot in close-up, he talks softly with controlled anger.

57

> CAMERON: 'What is it, a family? All those people gathered round, your own little make-believe family. You even had a baby just to finish it off. If you think that's a family then you're fucked. It's sex. It's always sex with you. Everything you do is sex. What do you think Vince is there for?'
> STUART: 'He's my friend.'
> CAMERON: 'He's just waiting. He's been waiting so long he thinks he's happy. Being with you every day of his life is as close as he's going to get.'

> STUART: 'Close to what?'
>
> CAMERON: 'To the day you finally turn around and fuck him. And don't tell me you didn't know that. Look, I could go, I could just walk away. I don't think he'd even notice. But he's worth the chance.'

These two clashes open up the hermetically sealed world of the series to outside criticism. Brief snide comments are made to Vince in early episodes by both Phil and Nathan regarding his doting dependency on Stuart, but this is the first time that Stuart has been directly attacked for sustaining that reliance. In addition, Cameron's utterances about 'make-believe families' raise the topic of what the concept of family might mean to queer individuals – and what a 'queer family' might constitute. That these subjects have been continuing concerns in lesbian/gay/queer politics and culture for many years once again connects the series with the lived politics of sexual difference.

Evidently, the parents of Nathan, Vince and Stuart play key roles in *Queer as Folk*. Hazel and Janice are supportive and protective of their gay sons. But Stuart's inability to come out to his parents – connected, possibly, to his Irish ancestry? – has led him to distance himself from them. Stuart's parents are represented as relatively warm-hearted. Stuart's father even hints, in episode six, that Stuart could talk to him about his problems ('If ever there's anything …', Clive says, but doesn't finish his sentence, or his offer). And yet moments of dialogue reveal Clive and Margaret as stubborn and conservative: as Stuart says to his sister Marie, referring to her ex, 'How long did you take to tell them that Robert was leaving? He was halfway down the M6!'. Finally, Roy Maloney's angry vengeful attack on Stuart's jeep, though understandable, prevents him from becoming a figure of sympathy. Indeed, Roy's continued inability to comprehend or tolerate his son's homosexuality leads, in episode eight, to a dramatic narrative moment for Nathan: referring to his daughter, Roy tells Nathan that 'as far as Helen's concerned, the anus is for shit'. This outburst finally provides the teenager with a justifiable reason for rejecting his biological family: he packs a bag, steals Roy's wallet, and takes a taxi to London with Donna.

But in addition to these parental figures, *Queer as Folk* presents a complex social network of queer characters (and some straight ones) who are deeply involved with each other's lives. The extended group of lesbians depicted – Lisa and Romey are often accompanied by their friends Siobhan and Suzie – regularly crosses paths with Vince, Stuart and their coterie, with Alfred operating as a linking social pivot to bring them all together. The series, through these characters, builds up what Kath Weston has called a 'family we choose'.[61] And in its inclusion of *actual* family members – Hazel, most notably – this group could be understood as a 'framily': that is, a support network incorporating both family members and friends. In this regard, it is worth comparing *Queer as Folk* to other drama series and comedies on television that also attempt to construct alternative queer family structures between their characters. David Fisher and Keith Charles in *Six Feet Under* (Greenblatt Janollari/Actual Size for HBO, 2001–5), for instance, sustain an (occasionally open) sexual relationship, and are committed to having children, whether adopted or delivered by a surrogate. The two men are supported throughout their parenting endeavours by the extended Fisher clan, a number of whom (especially Claire and Brenda) could be said to have queer identities. And in *Will and Grace* (Komut/Three Sisters/NBC, 1998–2006), disastrous heterosexuality (Grace's inability to find or keep a partner, Karen's lousy parenting, Will's parents' divorce) is set off against the enduring bonds of friendship between gay men and their female pals. The core group of characters is complicated and enlarged by attempts to include partners, such as Will's cop boyfriend Vince, and children, such as Jack's son Elliot.

59

Fictional film and television representations of 'families we choose' proliferated in the UK and US in the 1990s, and played a significant role in the mainstreaming of homosexuality. Taking their incentive from progenitors such as *thirtysomething* (Bedford Falls/MGM for ABC, 1987–91), programmes like *This Life*, *Friends*, *Melrose Place* (Darren Star/Spelling for Fox, 1992–9) and *Cold Feet* (Granada for ITV, 1997–2003), as well as films such as *Peter's Friends*

'Framily'

David and Keith in *Six Feet Under*

(1992) and *Reality Bites* (1994), featured extended social networks of supportive chums and biological kin. Often, these groups would include at least one gay character who would be depicted sympathetically, if usually as desexualised. Movies focused specifically on gay/queer framilies produced during this decade include *Longtime Companion* (1990), *Love! Valour! Compassion!* (1997) and *The Broken Hearts Club* (2000), while similar dynamics are evident in New Queer Cinema fare such as *Paris Is Burning* (1990), *Totally F***ed Up* and *Go Fish* (1994). Many of these titles attained widespread distribution and attention: in doing so, they disseminated the notion that 'families' do not have to be constituted solely of blood relations.

Cameron reveals through his argument with Stuart that he doesn't perceive the younger man's messy social network as a 'family'. Stuart, certainly, might just be playing at being grown up: Romey and Lisa operate as the primary caregivers, such that Stuart could walk away from Alfred's dirty nappies at any time (indeed, in episode three Stuart dumps the baby on Vince). Cameron accuses Stuart of narcissism, hedonism and of privileging his own self-gratification, hardly ideal qualities for a reliable, responsible parent. And Stuart makes it clear to Cameron in episode five that he isn't challenged by his job, and that he is flighty, restless and might abandon his home and friends and move to London. However, frustrated by Vince's unassailable dedication to Stuart, Cameron is unable to comprehend what might make Stuart attractive to his pals: that is, his unswerving plain-speaking, loyalty and devotion, firm political beliefs and actions, and boldness of spirit. Stuart may only dole out words of love and kindness on rare occasions – 'Just remember one thing. You're fantastic', he tells Vince as the latter walks to his first date with Cameron – but they're always genuine. In many ways the lead character of *Queer as Folk*, Stuart is also the most important and intriguing figure in its complicated extended 'family'. That Cameron doesn't like, understand or approve of this family only foreshadows what will happen to him by the end of the series.

The Stuart/Cameron wrangles continue in episode seven, which is focused almost entirely on Vince's thirtieth birthday party. This event is held in Stuart's flat, duly decked out for the occasion with streamers and balloons, and hung with Warhol-like screenprints of Vince's portrait. In its narrow focus, the episode resembles a one-act

61

Vince's thirtieth birthday party

62   play, echoing other gay dramas set at parties – in particular, it could be seen as an upbeat version of *The Boys in the Band* (which was made into a film by William Friedkin in 1970). At the bash, Stuart acts flirtatiously with Vince in order to wind Cameron up, and suggests to Vince that they could move in together. Cameron gives Vince a cheap car as a gift, but he is upstaged by Stuart: when Vince returns to Stuart's flat after a spin in the Mini, he is given a working model of K9, the robot dog from *Doctor Who*, a present with which he is clearly much more enamoured. Cameron, left out, swings the car keys from his finger. Later, Rosalie – one of Vince's colleagues at the supermarket, who has a crush on him – turns up at the party. Stuart has invited her on the sly; introduced to Cameron, she storms out, calling Vince 'a dirty little poof'. Stuart's behaviour is intentional: he tries to drive Vince away by acting obnoxiously. The morning after the party, Hazel gives Stuart back Vince's keys to Stuart's flat. Stuart dangles them from his finger in an echo of Cameron's stance with the Mini keys, highlighting their symbolic status as the keys to Vince's affections.

Identifying part seven as resembling a one-act *play* raises a
key concern about *Queer as Folk*: acting and performance styles.
This episode, in particular, allows the space for many of the cast to
display their acting skills. By situating most of its events in one location,
the focus of the audience is directed on the abilities of the actors to

63

Cameron and the Mini keys

Stuart and the keys to his flat

emote, to inhabit their characters believably, and so on. The first scene in the episode even self-reflexively identifies this. It hinges on Vince's acting: in the lift on the way up to Stuart's flat, he is practising faking an appropriate response ('Oh my God!') to the 'surprise' party he is about to enter. Yet Vince regularly uses the phrase 'Oh my God' throughout *Queer as Folk* – when the plastic torso is revealed in episode one, when he is talking to the man infested with Brazilian beach parasites in episode three … . Examined retrospectively, how many of those exclamations have also been faked or performed?

It is not my intention here to evaluate the performances of specific cast members, as personal responses to individual characters – and actors' abilities in portraying those characters – are likely to be (at least partly) subjective. However, looking at the acting in *Queer as Folk* more broadly, it is possible to make several observations. First, it is worth noting the extent to which the performances of many of the main actors in the series work against stereotypes associated with the depiction of queer individuals. The range of types used, historically, to represent gay/lesbian sexuality in film and television has been narrow: swishy and effeminate men, moustachioed clones, sad young men, masculine women, lipstick lesbians. Each of these types is marked by a limited vocabulary and grammar of gestures and expressions, tics and tropes, swiftly recognisable to the audience as signifiers of queer 'otherness'. Vince and Nathan rarely display aspects of these types, although both are a little 'soft'. With his clear skin, prominent facial mole and tousled blond hair, Nathan resembles a boy-band member (albeit one who is, as Dazz says in episode five, a 'dirty shagger'). Vince, in contrast, is self-effacing, unassuming, diffident, a perennial loser with a gentle voice, yet his clothes, accent and bumble also clearly identify him as a northern lad. Stuart flits between gendered styles of behaviour: he might play Leonardo to Vince's Kate, and aggressively snap 'I'll give you a fuck, you tight little virgin' at a schoolboy, but he also flirts coquettishly and emits high, rather feminine giggles. Lisa and Romey are both intelligent, attractive, middle-class lesbians. Although there are subtle differences between their characters – Lisa, who has shorter hair

64

Non-stereotypical lesbians

Alexander

than Romey, is more assertive, perhaps appropriate to her job as a solicitor – neither woman is 'glamorous' or 'masculine' (this despite the scripts describing Lisa as 'a classic lipstick lesbian'[62]). Notably, then, the dykes (Siobhan, most obviously) and camp boys (Alexander, Dane, Dazz) are relegated to more subsidiary roles – though, of course, each actor imbues the type they play with different degrees of depth, personality and disposition. Queeny Alexander, for instance, provides the expected pithy quips and outlandish outfits: at Vince's birthday party not only does he DJ ('Good evening, I'm Christine Cagney and I'm an alcoholic'), he also performs a short drag show clad in a maroon turban and spangly red top, lip-synching to the Spice Girls. And yet, as his disastrous 'relationship' with Lee and encounter with O'Hagan the mortician demonstrate, he *is* getting laid, and thus he counters the stereotypical association of campness with being sexless. In addition, his difficult relationship with his parents reveals a core of hurt beneath his bolshy persona. While out shopping in episode six, Alexander is ignored by his parents; he yells 'Hello? *Hello?* I said hello!' after them, but they glide away. A root of pain is thus exposed, one that becomes a significant narrative strand in *Queer as Folk 2*.

Second, the dominant performance mode in *Queer as Folk* is naturalistic, with characters constructed as coherent and believable, their personalities conveyed through repetitive elements of behaviour: Nathan's egotism and taste for drama, Vince's fibbing and self-sacrificing nature. This contrasts markedly with much queer independent cinema, in which performances are often self-conscious and deliberately false in order to draw attention to the fact that all behaviours and roles – whether 'real life' or filmed for the screen – are to some extent acted and inauthentic. From Holly Woodlawn in *Trash* (1970) to Divine in *Polyester* (1981), and from Bruce LaBruce's fake Warhol turn in his own *Super 8½* (1993) to Jackie Beat in *Grief* (1993), acting in queer screen culture is often purposefully stagy in order to expose the largely invisible or ignored parameters of 'realistic' performances. In doing so, alternative criteria for evaluating acting are brought into play: why are certain styles of performance rewarded with awards and commendations, while others are denigrated? In *Queer as Folk*, some characters behave flamboyantly (Alexander in particular) but this does not hinder their believability. In fact, only Stuart's behaviour lurches about unpredictably in a rather disconcerting manner. But rather than allying Aidan Gillen's performance with the strategic self-reflexive acting of queer artists such as Divine, Stuart's inconsistency, present at the level of the script, merely contributes to making him enigmatic and does not undermine the construction of his character.

Third – and this bears scrutiny due to the amount of publicity and comment it attracted at the time of the series' screening – almost all of the main cast of actors were heterosexuals playing gay. In fact, only Jonathon Natynczyk and Antony Cotton were openly gay actors. Promoting the series, the three leads were asked time and again by journalists what it was like being 'gay for pay', how difficult they had found playing queer characters, and what it was like kissing someone of the same sex. Commenting on the persistent repetition of these questions, Craig Kelly said that 'You feel like saying ... that that's what I do. I'm an actor. Actors play parts.' Charlie Hunnam also defended their casting: 'Just because you're not familiar with all this [Canal Street, this particularly "gay world"] doesn't mean you can't understand it.'[63] The cast and production personnel behind *Queer as Folk*, then, had to tackle widespread assumptions and prejudices regarding the abilities of actors to play characters of the same or a different sexual orientation (that is, that gay actors can only play gay, and that heterosexual actors will find playing gay difficult or disconcerting). What those making such assumptions failed to acknowledge was the complexity of the characters and performances in the series. To take just one example, Vince is closeted at work: in other words, heterosexual actor Craig Kelly had to play a fairly straight-acting gay character who, when *in situ* in Harlo's supermarket, acts heterosexual.

Fourth, *Queer as Folk* arguably demonstrates one of the distinguishing differences between acting for television and for cinema. John Caughie, writing about acting in television drama, has noted the medium's distinctive focus on detail:

> British television drama seems to me to have evolved as a drama of incident and character rather than as a drama of the kind of ruthlessly driven goal-oriented narrative which is associated with classic Hollywood cinema. It is

67

situation which holds the attention rather than the suspense of resolution, and it is recognition of characters in situations which forms the characteristic pleasure (not the universal pleasure) of television drama, rather than the fantasy of identification with ideal egos. [. . .] It is, in other words, a drama in which acting as detail plays a very particular part.[64]

Although *Queer as Folk* does provide some conclusions in its final episode, Caughie's quote seems pertinent to identifying some of the satisfactions of the series. *Queer as Folk* offers up a narrative peppered with incidental details, memorable scenes, moments and situations: individual lines of dialogue and their idiosyncratic delivery, sparky interactions, aspects of character delineated through looks, gestures, movement ... These could include – and I am aware that this list will reveal only my own particular delights in the series – Stuart's Liam Gallagher lollop down Canal Street as he tries to evade Nathan in episode two, Hazel's stagger as she brings Vince a cup of coffee near the end of the same instalment, Alexander's delivery of the word 'Nice' when he first surveys the mortician's flat in episode three, Donna's line 'I burnt the ham' in episode four. In fact, one of Russell T. Davies's specific skills as a writer, and one which particularly suits him to television, is his observational perspicacity: that is, his ability to capture the cadences of everyday speech. The skill of the cast lies in transforming his script into a series littered with detailed pleasures of performance. It is notable that the focus in the second half of the series on the mundane and quotidian, party rings and nappies, might allow audiences to identify these incidental textures and joys which the fireworks of the first four episodes somewhat obscure.

Even the final instalment of *Queer as Folk* retains the close concentration on conversation and incident. It does contain spectacular moments: Stuart drives a jeep he is test-driving through a plate-glass window at a dealership, Lance is taken away by the police after punching a representative from the Home Office in the face, and the episode ends with Vince and Stuart dancing on a podium to 'It's Raining Men', the camera craning up to the ceiling to occupy a position looking down at them. But other moments vital to the episode's narrative occur quietly in domestic or commonplace spaces. Nathan's confrontation with Roy happens in the kitchen (seemingly a key location in the Maloney household for dramatic interactions). Cameron, dressed only in his underwear, tells Vince he loves him as Vince sits in the bath scrubbing his own back with a loofah. Stuart and Vince reconcile over lunch; their interaction is so closely focused on their faces that the location is largely irrelevant. In their exchange, Stuart reifies the mundane: 'You've done nothing, Vince. You go to work, you go for a drink, you sit and watch cheap science fiction. Small and tiny world. What's so impressive about that, what's there to love? [...] It was good enough for me.' Ultimately, it is this 'tiny world' that wins out: Cameron is dumped, the Mini abandoned. The new life that Cameron might have given Vince, taking him away from the repetitions of the scene, is rejected in favour of the known and familiar.

While the Cameron/Vince/Stuart storyline unfolds throughout the second half of *Queer as Folk*, Nathan follows his own trajectory, which – a little like the teenager himself – is wayward and messy. At the start of episode five, he wakes up in the bed of unemployed Dazz –

Dazz, Nathan and Donna

according to the script, '19, a hard sort of camp, a Village boy'.[65] Dazz is cocky and swishy. He has been out on the scene for longer than Nathan, and has the arrogant mince and alarming wardrobe to prove it. Dazz's bedroom features a slogan poster that is mis-spelled – 'Smash the Facist Hetrosexual Orthodoxy' – which suggests an investment in queer politics, however cosmetic. (Nathan later uses the poster's phrase in a conversation with Donna during a school cross-country run, which merely exposes his bluster and naivety.) Nathan learns from Dazz, who offers some advice about Stuart: 'He's not young. And he knows it. Your age, you can make him beg.' Indeed, Nathan starts to rib Stuart about his advancing years: he offers to look after Alfred, adding 'Cos you're working all week, you must be worn out. At your age.' By the party in episode seven, Nathan is sidelining Donna in favour of Dazz, his new best pal; the two boys are planning to move into a council property together. 'Tell 'em you're gay and they give you a flat!' exclaims Nathan; 'Tell 'em your Dad's a queerbasher, you get a penthouse,' says Dazz. These comments – especially when considered alongside Romey and Lance's fake relationship, fabricated in order to attain Lance permanent residency, and Stuart's camped-up ditzy performance for two policemen in *Queer as Folk 2*, adopted to imply that a gay man would be incapable of committing an act of destruction – serve to make a subtle political point. That is, they highlight that queer individuals might pervert the state's system in order to attain their own ends. If the laws and regulations of a nation largely exclude or ignore you, or are even prejudiced against you, then the soft spots and loopholes of that system should be shaped and exploited to your benefit.

Dazz's flat is located on an estate dominated by tower blocks. In keeping with the focus on the ordinary and quotidian that Sarah Harding brings to the second half of *Queer as Folk*, the main locations used in episodes five to eight are domestic spaces, with brief glimpses afforded of the areas of Manchester in which these houses are situated. Stuart's parents' middle-class semi, Romey and Lisa's spacious home and suburban street, Hazel's tiny fenced back yard, open to the lane; although some of these spaces had been introduced in the first half of the series, the narrative dwells in them in the later episodes. Insights into character are offered through a spread of city locations, and the lived textures of Manchester beyond Canal Street and Vince and Stuart's apartments are opened up.

The late 1990s and early 2000s actually witnessed a proliferation of drama and comedy series on British television set in and around Manchester, including *Cold Feet*, *The Cops* (World Productions for the BBC, 1998–2000), *The Royle Family* (BBC, 1998–2006), *Queer as Folk*, *Clocking Off*, *Phoenix Nights* (Goodnight Vienna Productions for Channel 4, 2001–2), *Cutting It* (BBC, 2002–) and *Shameless*. Prior to the appearance of these programmes, the dominant representation of Manchester on British television had been provided, since 1960, by the soap opera *Coronation Street*. Set around the fictional town of Weatherfield, *Coronation Street*'s familiar locations – the roofs of the terraced houses seen in the programme's opening credits, the cobbled

71

Coronation Street's cobbles

streets, the central social hub of the Rovers Return, the cramped interiors of the houses, the local shop, and so on – construct a limited, rather claustrophobic geography through which the characters circulate. Although major soapy events occur in *Coronation Street* (murder, infatuation, affairs, transsexualism) the dominant tone of the programme is usually lightly comedic, centred on sparky dialogue and perceptive character observation. The programme has, of course, altered over the decades, though arguably not substantially: tales of working-class spirit and community, and flat vowels, continue to dominate.

Some of the more recent series have provided a broader sense of the size and sprawl of Manchester. *The Cops*, for instance, featured a significant amount of location shooting, but tended to emphasise – in stark contrast to *Coronation Street* – the relentless misery of living in the city. The bobbies themselves were mostly bitter, violent, prejudiced, barely holding it together. Shot with shaky hand-held cameras, the run-down estates the police were called out to, and the city-centre sites in which they broke up squabbles, were tawdry, grey, tired. *Shameless* revisits a number of these locations – it is centred on the working-class Chatsworth estate – but offers up a diametrically opposed view of the city. In this version of Manchester, the houses may have boarded-up windows and yards full of detritus, but their interior décor is colourful and vibrant, and their inhabitants make them welcoming spaces, with social events kicking off at unpredictable times. Shots of tower blocks, burntout cars, scraggy scrubland and concrete alleys are often edited together in a jaunty manner to Murray Gold's bouncy score, the series marked by its anarchic energy.

Queer as Folk also contains a great deal of outdoor location shooting. Partly, this needs to be understood as a response by Russell T. Davies to the restrictions he had endured in previous years:

> it was the first time since my early days in Children's [television] that I was allowed to write location-based drama. I was taken out of the studio (even *The Grand* was trapped in a Blue Shed in the Granada car park). It's no wonder the *Queer as Folk* characters keep running and driving and standing on roof tops. I was free![66]

The Cops: Manchester as bleak and depressing

Shameless: Manchester as vibrant

But the depiction of Manchester that appears in *Queer as Folk* is strikingly distinct. Utilising a strong colour palette, bold framing and mobile cameras, key locations become fantastical spaces, especially in episodes one to four of the series. In the first episode, for instance, the hospital in which Alfred is born is a palace of glass and light, bearing little relation to the working environments of *Casualty* (BBC, 1986–) or *Holby City* (BBC, 1999–). The brief shots in the airport at the beginning of episode three, depicting reflective metal surfaces and a sense of hygienic cleanliness, resemble scenes from science-fiction films such as *The Island* (2005). Stuart's apartment, as was highlighted in Chapter 1, seems more like a show-home than an environment that anyone actually inhabits. And as Vince approaches his first date with Cameron in episode five, he crosses a bridge lit in strong blues and purples, a location that looks as though it is on loan from a pop video or a high-budget game-show. But the most fantastical location in *Queer as Folk* is Canal Street: the colours, lights and framing of Via Fossa, Mantos, Babylon and the cobbled street itself construct the spaces of Manchester's gay scene as a seductive utopia.[67] The glossy depiction of all of these places needs to be set against the series' investment in revealing the reality and complexity of queer life: this is a world that has never been shown on television before, but it is also presented in a fictional context – and sometimes that fiction is patently obvious. Ultimately, *Queer as Folk*'s arresting representation of specific parts of Manchester had an allure that impacted on the city itself: according to newspaper reports, the tourist influx to Canal Street (often of groups of straight women) boomed in the wake of the series.

Of course, there are also a host of locations – from Nathan's family home to Hazel's street, from the straight pub in episode two to the path where Donna and Nathan have their cross-country run in episode five – that are shot more 'realistically', and that thus seem more mundane, less significant. And yet, as the second half of the series reveals in particular, dramatic incident does not need to occur in hyperbolised or stylised surroundings. While eating cheese in Romey and Lisa's kitchen (and it is worth noting that a great deal of cheese is eaten in *Queer as Folk*: Donna is particularly keen on dairy), Cameron discovers, through a conversation with Lisa, that Vince is besotted with Stuart: 'It's the greatest love story never told,' she says. And the confrontation between Stuart and Roy Maloney takes place on a deserted and unremarkable street. Stuart, aggravated by a trip to see his own parents, delivers Nathan home, telling the teenager to make amends with his family. His jeep is rammed from behind: Roy has driven into Stuart's vehicle. The drama of the situation – heightened by the charged exchange that follows, and the fact that Stuart is dressed in his full Satan outfit of black suit, dark shiny shirt and red tie – is rendered realistic and involving through the drab location and the stark daylight in which the scene is shot. Incidental details of set and costume serve to further ground the sequence in the everyday: Nathan's younger sister Helen, for instance, wears a large pair of white bunny slippers.

Nathan escapes from Roy in Stuart's jeep. In later episodes, he repays Stuart by breaking up Romey and Lance's fake relationship, and by engineering episode eight's reconciliation between Stuart and Vince, these interventions partly motivated by his continuing adoration of the older man. And yet he struggles with his own political agency, as two scenes in the final episode of the series demonstrate. In the first, Nathan sits and suffers through anti-gay comments during a class at school on Wilfred Owen. In an oblique reference to Clause 28, the UK legislation introduced by Thatcher's government in 1988 that outlawed the 'promotion of homosexuality' by local authorities, school bully Christian Hobbs (the perpetrator of a homophobic beating in episode four) points out to the teacher that 'You can't teach us about poofs, it's not allowed.' The teacher replies: 'it's nothing to do with the man's poetry. Though no doubt he found plenty of things to do in the trenches other than fight.' But knowledge of Owen's sexuality is vital for understanding his poetry, and for providing students with some notion of a history of queer individuals. In addition, the comment on gay men's 'inappropriate' sexual behaviour during warfare calls to mind some of the discriminatory rhetoric and commentary that circulated in the US (and beyond) when Clinton's administration introduced their 'Don't Ask, Don't Tell' policy for the military in 1993. This short scene, in other words, manages to highlight both the persistence of a Thatcherite policy that meant teachers across the UK were afraid to talk to their students about matters of queer sexuality, and the widespread assumptions and insinuations that gay men cannot operate within the military. In the second scene, set in the New Union, Nathan and Donna spot Hobbs, there with trophy girlfriend Cathy Mott. (Davies evidently likes this surname: there is a Suzie Mott in *Bob and Rose*, and a Debbie Mott in the one episode of *Linda Green* [Red for BBC, 2001–2] he wrote.) Nathan takes to the stage to sing karaoke, the opening bars of 'I Should Be So Lucky' emanating from the speakers, but actually stops the music and humiliates Christian: 'That boy there. He beats us up cos we're queer.' Davies is critical of the generic feel-good nature of this scene: 'I'd see films where people do things like this and I'd sit and go "what a piece of shit". Then I write it myself!'.[68] But following on from the Wilfred Owen scene, which demonstrated Nathan's impotency in the public setting of a school classroom, Hobbs's shaming works to reveal the necessity of gay bars as supportive and safe locations, and thus the continued political need for segregated spaces.

For his part, Stuart's political agency is assured. Two sequences in the second half of *Queer as Folk* highlight Stuart's position

76

Martin Brooks and Stuart

as the most overtly politicised character in the series. In episode five, he is asked by his company to wine and dine a businessman called Martin Brooks, in order to get Brooks to sign a contract. Brooks – played by Michael Culkin, although the producers initially wanted Timothy Spall for the role – is married, middle-aged, overweight. Rather than a trip to see *Twelfth Night*, Brooks requests a night out on the scene with Stuart, where he attempts to blackmail the younger man into having sex with him: 'I'll sign the contract. If you're prepared to …'. (Blackmail reappears as a substantial plot element in *Queer as Folk 2*.) Stuart pretends that Vince is his boyfriend, and instead sets Brooks up with another patron in Via Fossa. The next morning, Brooks suggests to Stuart that he'd like to cancel his train and stay longer. Stuart snaps back:

> Fine. Cancel. Go out, get pissed, get shagged. Then you can do it again, then you can do it again. Get shagged every night of your life. Forget your wife, forget your kids. Just don't be a tourist. You either do it or you don't. So what's it going to be – staying or going?

77

The accusation of cultural tourism stings, and produces a result: Brooks leaves. Stuart's worldview is clearly on display here. His angry tone suggests the bravery it takes to commit to a queer identity and lifestyle: it is not acceptable, he seems to say, for ostensibly straight people (or closeted bisexuals and gay men, hiding within 'normal' families) to indulge in a bit of 'exotic' queer fun every so often, only to then return to their nominally heterosexual lives.

The second sequence appears in episode eight. Going slightly off the rails after falling out with Vince at the latter's birthday party, Stuart shops for a new jeep. The salesman advises him against one specific make because of its queer appeal: 'We get a lot of gay guys buying this one … . Thing about those lads, money to burn. Then they die young, so we get the resale value.' Stuart, riled, takes the jeep for a spin – straight through the plate-glass window of the showroom. This sequence is shot partly from the salesman's point of view behind his desk, and partly from Stuart's perspective. As the glass hits the

Stuart's point of view through the jeep windscreen ...

... as he smashes through the showroom window

windscreen, the salesman jumps and cowers: the audience at home, should they wish, is enabled to occupy Stuart's position, and to experience the proxy thrill of his actions. This sequence operates as both a satisfying moment of extravagant spectacle, and as an instance of direct political retaliation against a homophobic individual. However, the politics of interventionist activism are not properly debated until *Queer as Folk 2*.

Of course, the end of episode eight – and of the series – sees Vince and Stuart reunited, Stuart once more grounded by his pal and thus, possibly, prevented from repeating such destructive behaviour. Russell T. Davies has commented of the end of *Queer as Folk*: 'It's so perverse. He [Vince] gives it all up for unrequited love.'[69] This quote actually raises a number of issues regarding narrative form and audience pleasure – and what, indeed, a 'perverse' narrative might look, sound and feel like. If *Queer as Folk* had been a movie, would Stuart have died (perhaps as moral punishment for his sins), and Vince have ended up with Cameron? (As Vince runs to Canal Street at the end of the final episode, Stuart is close to picking up Harvey, the man responsible for Phil's overdose death in episode three.) Would a monogamous pairing for Vince have provided a 'happy ending', and a form of character growth, more suited to cinema?

The conclusion of *Queer as Folk* exalts in bonds of friendship over romantic stability, in unrequited love over satiation, in the pleasures of the same old gay scene rather than new horizons. The two male leads finish the series very close to where they started off – in Babylon, on Canal Street, dancing intimately but not fucking – albeit a little bit wiser, perhaps a little more balanced in their relationship to each other. This ending makes sense with regards to a serialised drama: not only does it suggest the potential for a sequel, for further stories and series featuring the same characters, but it also reveals the delights of repetition that fire, in part, the continued consumption of the episodic. For, unlike the one-off text (whether novel, play or film) which usually provides some sort of closure, many serialised fictions (comic books, television series) never reach an adequate conclusion, or delay their conclusions for as long as possible. Indeed, when significant narrative development or closure does occur in episodic formats, it may disrupt the pleasures of repetition: witness, for instance, how the textures and satisfactions provided by *Frasier* altered once the unrequited relationship between Niles and Daphne became overt. *Queer as Folk*, of course, *does* conclude: episode eight actually contains ending after ending. Some of these conclusions provide closure: Lance's deportation, Cameron's binning. But others – Nathan and Donna's taxi ride to London, that final podium dance – open up the possibility of further tales. That is, these are 'season finale' conclusions: satisfying in their own right, while also inviting audiences to speculate as to what might happen next. This ending, then, is no more 'perverse' than many other examples of serial television drama, echoing as it does the format adopted by other writers (and their series' conclusions) who may wish to keep open the worlds of their creation.

Within each individual episode of *Queer as Folk*, the narrative structure adopted is also one with which audiences of contemporary television drama are familiar. Short, punchy scenes of a minute or two in length, several storylines edited together in a choppy, speedy manner – this is what Robin Nelson has termed 'flexi-narrative'. This televisual storytelling form, Nelson argues, in which narrative resolution of any individual story strand may not occur, is clearly indebted to the complexity and open-endedness of the soap opera; it is a form, he suggests, which responds to and reflects the complexities and uncertainties of contemporary Western society.[70] Although its aesthetic presentation may vary somewhat from programme to programme (more or less saturated colours, mobile cameras, distinctive editing techniques and so on), the flexi-narrative form can be identified in operation in a host of television drama series, from *EastEnders* to *Shameless*.

But what is perverse about *Queer as Folk* – and, indeed, one of the reasons that the series was markedly original and deserves its place within a canon of television classics – is the challenge that it posed, in terms of its storytelling, to earlier narratives that featured queer characters. Lesbian and gay characters had almost always been peripheral to television drama: subsidiary figures occupying specific roles. As Dennis Allen has pointed out in an article on *Melrose Place*, that series could only include gay character Matt Fielding (Doug Savant) if a new 'coming-out' narrative could be constructed for him; that is, his narrative role was simply to reveal or confess his homosexuality to another character.[71] Queer characters are still often constructed this way for television, with the revelation of their sexuality serving as their primary narrative role: as recent examples, see Todd Grimshaw (Bruno Langley) in *Coronation Street*, quickly written out after coming out, or Adam (Philip Olivier) in *Hollyoaks: In the City* (Mersey Television for E4, 2006). Anna McCarthy, in an essay on *Ellen* (ABC, 1994–8), has suggested that the problem lies not just with the stories told, but with television itself: the medium's regular formats, its routine scheduling and its predictable structures cannot accommodate the marginality, the liminality, of queer sexualities.[72] Judith Roof has even argued that the problem is narrative *per se*: in her book *Come As You Are*, she links narrative as a totalising system to both capitalist ideologies and heterosexuality.[73]

 Queer as Folk problematises all of these arguments, troubles at their foundations. For although it featured coming-out scenes, and although it clearly functioned as a marketable piece of programming within the schedule of a commercial television network, it also – week after week – presented boldly, uncompromisingly queer characters and narratives to its audience. Regardless of how satisfying individual audience members may (or may not) have found the ending of *Queer as Folk*, the series definitively demonstrated that queer characters could be placed centre-stage within an episodic drama, that enjoyable and entertaining narratives could be told about queer lives, and that space could be made within the medium of television for regular stories about queer sexualities.

3 A Shot to the Head

Over the course of its airing, the first series of *Queer as Folk* picked up a regular audience of several million viewers, and a number of television critics, including *Time Out*'s Alkarim Jivani and *Gay Times*'s Megan Radclyffe, heaped substantial praise on the show. Bootleg copies of *Queer as Folk* swiftly circulated internationally, increasing the size of the series' fan base. Screenings at lesbian and gay film festivals outside the UK were rapturously received: at Los Angeles' Outfest in July 1999, for instance, according to Kristin Hohenadel, 'almost all of the 600 mostly gay men stayed in their seats – laughing, cheering and clapping along to the catchy theme tune – for the 4½ hours of back-to-back episodes'.[74] Also in July of 1999 Channel 4's chief executive, Michael Jackson, wrote an article for the *Guardian* in which he pinpointed *Queer as Folk* as emblematic of what the channel was doing, and what it could be:

> The programme I think sums up our aspirations is *Queer as Folk*. It was funny, truthful and stylish. In the past, this subject would have been handled in a self-conscious manner. But in *Queer as Folk* there are no 'issues'. There are only emotions, unsympathetic gay characters and, shockingly, no safe-sex message. It's a programme no other broadcaster would have shown.[75]

The series spawned profitable merchandising opportunities for Channel 4 in the form of video and DVD releases, soundtrack CDs and a book of unexpurgated scripts. In a December issue of the American magazine *Entertainment Weekly*, Ken Tucker called *Queer as Folk* 'the best series you'll probably never see', noting that the Stuart/Nathan sex scene in episode one 'was enough to consign it to gay film festivals and bootlegged Internet video sales over here'.[76] Rounding out the year, the cover of Channel 4's annual report for 1999 featured an image of Aidan Gillen alongside pictures of Ali G and two of the cast members from the Channel 4-financed film *East Is East*. In the report, *Queer as Folk* was identified by Michael Jackson as one of 'a number of signature shows [screened in 1999] that commanded ratings, plaudits and a place in the wider cultural debate'.[77]

With this level of cultural recognition, and of support from audiences, critics and industry personnel, it is perhaps unsurprising that Channel 4 commissioned a second series of *Queer as Folk*. Initially, they asked Russell T. Davies for ten hour-long episodes – a more substantial series than the first run. But it was not to be:

> I did write that first hour, and if I ever told you what happened between
> Stuart and Vince's father, you'd never believe it … . But right from the start,
> my heart wasn't in it. I didn't want this to continue. A story should
> tell the one, special time in a character's life. Invent new stories, and
> you're saying that all their times are special, and I don't believe that.
> The connections binding Stuart, Vince and Nathan together were already
> failing. How long would two thirty-year-olds stay friends with a teenager?
> That aborted first script already had Nathan moving back into Hazel's,
> repeating his actions of Series 1, just to keep the strands connected.
> Big red science-fiction warning signs were flashing in my head. I kept quiet,
> mainly because I had ten hours' work to complete. But as ever, Nicola, Gub
> and Catriona were ahead of me. Over dinner …, Gub said the best words of
> all. 'Let's end it.' Oh, the relief.[78]

83

What *Queer as Folk 2* then became, in fact, was a script for a one-off two-hour-long 'special'. This 'film' – somewhat akin, perhaps, to a television play – would have opened with Vince and Stuart in Arizona

holding a gun to a man's head, and then proceeded to flashbacks, to
relate to audiences how the two leads had ended up in this situation.
Filming took place between 4 October and 7 November 1999. But
somewhere between the submission of the script and the final edit of the
programme, *Queer as Folk 2* became two hour-long episodes.
Comments made by Nicola Shindler and Russell T. Davies suggest that
there were some eleventh-hour editing decisions made regarding which
incidents and narrative threads should appear, or take precedence, in
which episode: Davies has even argued that the sequel 'never survived
being cut in half'.[79] Channel 4 marketed the programme as a key text in
its new year schedule: teaser and trailer television adverts were
accompanied by billboard hoardings showing the triumphant trio
against an orange background, with the cheeky slogan 'Same Men –
New Tricks' promising, at the very least, more queer sex. *Queer as Folk 2*
was broadcast in a 10pm slot on 15 and 22 February 2000.

    Queer as Folk 2 is a significantly different beast to the original
series. Partly, this is an issue of narrative form. In contrast to forty-
minute instalments, hour-long episodes of a drama need a different

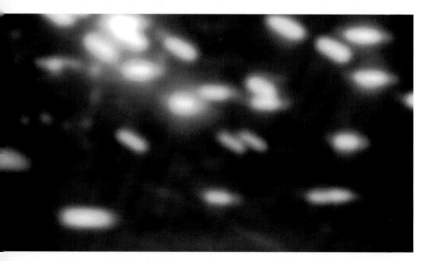

Queer as Folk 2's credits

rhythm to sustain audience attention. And a two-part drama requires a certain economy of scale and tightness of plotting that a longer series does not need to be so cautious about. (Davies would later return to the two-part form with *The Second Coming* in 2003.) The different character of *Queer as Folk 2* is also connected to alterations in style. The short credits sequence, for instance, has an alternative colour scheme. In place of the radiant oranges and reds of season one, the dominant colours are now yellow and black, autumnal rather than summer hues, suggesting a darker, more melancholy tone to the sequel. The new director, Menhaj Huda, largely abandoned the 'blurred lights' background that was a signature of the first series, and enhanced the gaudiness of specific locations: the bars and clubs, for instance, are riots of colour. He also utilised more hand-held camera to provide certain scenes with energy – there are conversations between characters in *Queer as Folk 2* shot in a style reminiscent of *This Life*, the camera ricocheting swiftly between faces without editing. The second episode of the sequel, in particular, looks different to the first episode and the entirety of the original series, due to the utilisation of specific stylistic devices. These include: snap zooms, in both directions, between mid-shots and close-ups on characters' faces; back-projection work in two sequences' (one in the nightclub Dantes, one on Canal Street); time-lapse dissolves; and a long sequence shot in slow motion (slow motion is rarely used in the first series, and then only fleetingly, as with Nathan and Stuart's cruising of each other in episode one). It is as though the regular syntax and textures of the series are fraying at the seams. In this respect, the conclusion of the sequel, which launches *Queer as Folk 2* into the realms of science fiction/fantasy, should perhaps not come as too much of a surprise.

Behind the scenes, there were other personnel changes: among others, Pam Tait was replaced as costume designer by Michael Johnson, cinematographer Alasdair Walker took over from Nigel Walters, and production designer Claire Kenny's shoes were filled by Jeff Tessler. In terms of the cast, additional people vanished: in fact, none of the original actors were placed under option to return in the event of a sequel. Of the lesbian couple from series one, only Romey reappeared, in one short café scene. Carla Henry (Donna) was not available for the shoot. An early sequence in *Queer as Folk 2* featuring Nathan and Donna being delivered back home by police after their sojourn in London used a replacement actress for Donna, who was only shot from behind; the scene was cut from the broadcast version of the series.

However, perhaps the most marked difference between the original *Queer as Folk* and the sequel is one of tone: *Queer as Folk 2* is a much angrier piece of drama. Stuart is blackmailed by his young nephew Thomas, leading to Stuart's coming out to his parents in a lengthy and confrontational monologue. Alexander's father has a stroke, and his mother asks him to sign away his inheritance rights, which he does. Alexander subsequently overdoses on pills, leading Stuart, in retaliation, to blow up Alexander's mother's car. Nathan confronts a teacher at his school who is ignoring the homophobic comments of other students in the classroom. Other incidents of casual anti-gay prejudice from peripheral characters appear throughout *Queer as Folk 2*. Mrs Fletcher, Vince's female boss at Harlo's, for instance, invites him to a party, then adds 'Mind you, it's a party every night for you lot, isn't it?'. At a wedding party, the bridegroom, Adrian, suggests that Vince being gay is 'a waste', to which Stuart angrily responds 'What's a waste exactly? [. . .] What, a waste of cock, waste of spunk, waste of a fuck, what? And you, you're not wasted, you get *vagina* ...'. And Vince's Dad, Dudley, describes all gay men as 'such good company, never short of a joke; tremendous wit, all of them. They're always smiling, they're always laughing', a stereotypical observation which elicits Hazel's sardonic reply, 'Yes, and they make such good pets.'

This angry tenor seems to have been a response by Davies to the reception of the first series of *Queer as Folk*. Interviewed for *Gay Times*, Davies discussed handling the publicity for, and controversy provoked by, the first eight episodes and how this affected the gestation of the content of *Queer as Folk 2*:

Over the past year, it has struck me that the defining factor of homosexuality is homophobia. It's not the fact that we sleep with people of the same sex, which is the obvious definition, because actually that definition wouldn't mean anything if there was no response *against* it. Because I've been coming across that homophobia in subtle forms and in bold forms every day over the past eight months, a lot of that has come out in the script.[80]

Elsewhere, Davies later elaborated on the specifics of that homophobia.

I'd spent months talking to lame journalists ('Surely no one has a problem with gay people any more? I have two gay friends who come to dinner parties, and they say everything's fine now'). I'd appeared on badly produced radio-debates ('Gay people should all be sent to live on an island. Not a bad island, they could have tennis courts and things'). I'd met dangerous fools ('I taught in a girls' school for forty years and none of them was lesbian'). One caller on Radio 5 told me off for laughing at the tennis court man: I told her that if I didn't laugh at this stuff, I'd be angry every day of my life.[81]

It is also possible that the anger of *Queer as Folk 2* was a response to the social and political climate in Britain following the screening of the first series. As noted in the introduction, on Tuesday 13 April 1999, the same day that episode eight of the first series was aired, the Sexual Offences (Amendment) Bill, which would have lowered the gay age of consent from eighteen to sixteen, and which had been passed by the House of Commons, was sabotaged in the House of Lords – primarily by the Conservative Baroness Young. (In November 2000, the Labour government had to invoke the Parliament Act, for only the fourth time since World War I, in order to bypass the House of Lords and equalise the age of consent at sixteen for heterosexuals and homosexuals.) April 1999 also witnessed three nail-bomb attacks in London: the first in Brixton, on 17 April; the second on Brick Lane, on 24 April; and the third on the Admiral Duncan, a gay pub in Soho, on 30 April. In the latter, sixty-five people were injured, and two killed. On 1 May 1999, twenty-two-year-old David Copeland was arrested in Cove, Hampshire, for perpetrating the attacks. And in the meantime, charged discussions

about the continued existence of Section 28 rumbled on: the legislation
that forbade the 'promotion of homosexuality' was only finally repealed
in November 2003 (although Scotland did away with the clause in June
2000).

The political tensions and conflicts were not just in the UK, of
course. Perhaps most significantly, in October 1998, during the filming
of the first series of *Queer as Folk*, Matthew Shepard was killed in
Laramie, Wyoming. Davies has made the connection to Shepard's
homophobic murder explicit in his comments on *Queer as Folk 2*, and
the transplanting of Vince and Stuart to Arizona at the end of the series:

> like a dark undertow from October '98 onwards, Matthew Shepard's story
> was on the news. The pickets at his funeral. Faggots Burn in Hell. Now go
> and watch Stuart Jones blow up that car. Watch him blow that fucker to
> hell. Of course he went to the Wild West – he went to find those placard-
> waving bastards. Good luck to him.[82]

This incensed tone, and the threat of violence, was apparent even in the
publicity for *Queer as Folk 2*: the tagline 'Back with a Bang' was used to
accompany teasers and trailers, the phrase suggesting both sexual

Vince with pricing gun

Stuart shapes his hand like a gun at the wedding reception

Stuart's hand-pistol

Stuart with an actual gun in Arizona

content and incendiary events. But they were woven into the very fabric of the sequel. There are several appearances of a gun motif: Vince pretends to shoot Graham, an obsequious middle manager at Harlo's who is also in line for promotion, with a pricing gun; at Vince's half-sister Judith's wedding reception, Stuart invites Vince to dance with him, holding out a hand with two fingers extended; and at the hospital where Alexander signs away his inheritance, Stuart threatens Alexander's mother with a similar 'hand gun', and presses the barrel – his first and second fingers – against her head. In the final 'Arizona' sequence of the sequel, these imaginary pistols are replaced by a real one.

The transposition of Vince and Stuart to America could be read as a comment on the exporting of *Queer as Folk* to the US (of which, more in the next chapter): the UK stories about Vince and Stuart are now over, but their adventures continue overseas. The sequence might also suggest that, by the end of the sequel, they have outgrown the UK, and that they have confronted head-on all of the problems and issues their native country has to throw at them. Certainly, the politics of *Queer as Folk 2* are more overt than in the original series. The sequel re-engages with some topics explored in *Queer as Folk*, including the age of consent and the racial politics of queer culture. But it also takes on other concerns in depth: blackmail, coming out, the relationship of gay men to their parents, direct-action activism, the queerness of genre. Throughout its exploration of all of these subjects, the Stuart/Vince/Nathan triangle continues, its tensions searching for an adequate form of resolution. In what follows here, I will use this range of topics to structure my discussion of the sequel.

The age of consent, as noted in Chapter 1, was a vital issue in the original *Queer as Folk* in relation to the narrative construction of a sexually aware queer adolescent, and his desire for relations with an older man. In the sequel, this topic is further commented on in two key scenes. At Judith's wedding reception, Hazel, Vince, Stuart and Alexander sit around a table listening to Vince's father Dudley as he gives a speech to the assembled throng. Hazel reveals to her gay coterie that she only had sex with the man once, in Piccadilly Gardens, when she was fifteen. 'Pervert! I mean, who'd sleep with a fifteen-year-old?' she asks. Stuart, the target of her sardonic comment, uses his mouth to waggle his cigar in a Groucho Marx manner. Hazel's rhetorical question raises the spectre of the controversy that surrounded episode one of the first series, and offers a challenge to critics. Would a television drama that featured a girl aged fifteen having sex with a twenty-nine-year-old male – which would similarly constitute statutory rape – have been received less hysterically? In a later scene, shortly after Stuart has come out to his parents, Hazel, Janice and Stuart's mother, Margaret, chat around Hazel's kitchen table. Hazel reveals to Margaret that she has known about Vince and Stuart being gay since they were fourteen. Janice states that she knew about Nathan when he was eleven and points out that, to the trained eye, a young boy's queerness can be evident at a very early age: 'When I'm on supply teaching, you go into a school, and there's a boy, just sitting there. And it's *shining* out of him.' Not only does this line reveal Janice as a liberal and sympathetic individual, but it kicks against the arbitrary nature of the age of consent, suggesting that a child's sexual identity may be formed and clear to see well before any legally imposed age limit.

Queer as Folk 2 also faces up to the issue of race: following criticisms of the original series for focusing at length on a group of almost exclusively white characters (with Donna the only major exception), the sequel contains two sequences that feature non-white actors. But both are problematic for those looking for 'positive' images of black characters. Considering the first series' attack on positive images of homosexuality, this is perhaps appropriate; however, it troubles any attempts at reparation. In episode two, the teacher that ignores (and thus is complicit in) the homophobic bullying of Nathan is black. Having suffered through the Wilfred Owen homophobic incident in series one, Nathan's behaviour in this sequence suggests that his trip to London boosted his self-confidence. Kids respond to the reading of their names on the register by calling 'here'; when Nathan's name is called, he confidently says 'queer' (a brave adoption of this label, clearly affiliated to both the graffiti-marked jeep of series one and Stuart's

coming-out speech). When the teacher chastises Nathan, the teenager
wonders aloud how come 'they say it and you don't say a thing'.
Speaking in a measured and quiet voice, Nathan dares the teacher
'to make something out of this, sir' – but the tutor backs down, and
continues reading the register.

Nathan's black teacher

Mickey Smith

The other notable non-white character in *Queer as Folk 2* appears in episode one's pre-credits scene: Vince and Stuart have brought a third party, Mickey Smith, back to Stuart's flat for sex. Mickey asks 'So is that what you do then – threesomes?', and requests not to be used as 'an extra cock'. The kissing starts, but Vince fails to get aroused. Uncomfortable, he scarpers using a fabricated tale about a neighbour being burgled, revealing that, despite playing along with the notion of a threesome, he has altered little since the end of the first series. Stuart is left to have his way with the third party. Mickey is merely a narrative tool, a pawn placed between Vince and Stuart to reintroduce their continuing unresolved sexual tensions. (The possibility of an alternative threesome – between Stuart, Vince and Nathan – is proposed by Stuart in the second episode. How many viewers had already fantasised this possibility? Nathan says that he's 'up for anything', but Vince snaps that he would 'rather have a wank'.) Of course, at the level of casting, the racial identities of Mickey and the homophobic teacher are irrelevant, their presence seemingly tokenistic. But the fact that both characters are present merely to get fucked – or fucked over – shifts their narrative positioning from incidental characters to sorely limited roles. As with the first series and its treatment of Lee and Lance, *Queer as Folk 2* suggests that there is little space in the lives of its characters for non-white individuals – and thus reinforces a comment made by film director Bruce LaBruce: 'Although lip service has been paid to miscegenation in the form of an occasional blow job, "queer" remains primarily a snow movement.'[83]

93

Aside from the topics of the age of consent and race, *Queer as Folk 2* also engages with other ethical and political concerns. Explorations of blackmail and coming out are woven together in the sequel's narrative, in confrontations between Stuart and his wicked nephew Thomas (a direct descendant, perhaps, of Rhoda in *The Bad Seed* [1956]). Early in the first episode, Stuart's sister Marie leaves her two kids with him at his flat. This is a new apartment located on Canal

Street itself, decorated in oranges and blues, glass panelling and ambient lighting – all still very *Wallpaper** magazine. While Stuart plays Scalextric with Benjamin, the younger sibling, Thomas uses Stuart's computer. 'It's good this, "Big Cock City"' says Thomas, and Stuart races to unplug the machine. (Incidentally, 'Big Cock City' is an actually existing website: its title page now proclaims 'As Featured on Stuart's PC!'). Thomas, realising that Stuart's parents don't know about his sexuality, demands £25 not to tell. Stuart responds by flushing Thomas's head down the toilet. Thomas, blubbing, demands more money and ups the ante, playing on the cultural associations often made between homosexuality and paedophilia: 'I'm telling my Dad, cos he wants access … . I'm telling him you touched me … . You pervert – you bloody pervert!' The appearance of this narrative recalls other fictional tales concerning homosexuality and blackmail, including the films *Victim* (1961) and *Advise and Consent* (1962).

Stories involving blackmail and queerness almost inevitably incorporate spectacular coming-out scenes: witness the climactic 'I *wanted* him' speech by Melvin Farr (Dirk Bogarde) in *Victim*. True to form, Thomas's threats lead to Stuart's striking coming out. This is, in fact, one of the only coming-out scenes in *Queer as Folk*. (Vince comes out to Marcie at Harlo's in the last episode of series one: she is so shocked that she can't shut her gaping mouth.) The relative lack of such scenes – a hardy staple of gay dramas, almost always followed by tears and recrimination, or statements of support and love – marks *Queer as Folk* as different from previous representations of homosexuality. Stuart's revelatory speech is audacious: round at Marie's new flat, she and her kids are involved in unpacking, with the help of Marie and Stuart's parents. Thomas starts to drop hints about 'men, lots of them', hanging around at Stuart's flat. Stuart's Dad asks for a hand with putting together a piece of flatpack furniture, but Stuart replies that he can't, because 'we don't do hammers or nails or saws. We do joints and screws, but that's different.' 'Who does?' asks his mother. 'Queers,' her son replies, and then delivers a lengthy monologue in a low, steady voice, looking directly at Thomas:

Thomas the blackmailing nephew

Stuart's coming-out moment

Because I'm queer. I'm gay. I'm homosexual. I'm a poof, I'm a poofta, I'm a ponce, I'm a bumboy batty-boy backside artist bugger. I'm bent, I am that arse bandit. I lift those shirts. I'm a faggot-arsed fudge-packing shit-stabbing uphill gardener. I dine at the downstairs restaurant. I dance at the other end of the ballroom. I'm Moses and the parting of the red cheeks.

I fuck and I'm fucked. I suck and I'm sucked. I rim them and wank them and every single man's had the fucking time of his life. And I'm not a pervert. If there's one twisted bastard in this family it's this little blackmailer here. So congratulations Thomas: I've just officially outed you.

The speech is shot in one long take, the camera gradually moving in towards Stuart. Setting is vital here: surrounded by the mess of unpacking, Stuart causes an emotional mess by unpacking the vocabulary of homosexuality. The twist of his monologue is in the last sentence: although the speech works as a hyperbolic confession regarding Stuart's sexuality, it transpires that the actual 'outing' is of Thomas as a nefarious nephew. Of course, the monologue *does* also name Stuart as a homosexual, but rather than the predictable 'Mum, Dad: I'm gay' emotive blurt, Stuart instead calmly identifies himself with a lengthy list of terms and phrases used colloquially (and often pejoratively) to refer to gay men. This does not upset him; it is simply a list, a description, a statement of fact.[84] *Queer as Folk* largely maintains a believable, realistic narrative and tone throughout its run, but two sequences in *Queer as Folk 2* in particular – this monologue, and the departure of Vince and Stuart from Canal Street in the final episode – shatter the illusion, rip open the text, and reveal to the audience that they are consuming a work of fiction. Although it is possible to interpret Stuart's speech as indicative of his tendency to excess, his predilection for the spectacular, it also serves as a moment of authorial rupture, a scene when Russell T. Davies's voice as the writer of the series can be heard over Stuart's own.

As this scene highlights, the relationships between gay men and their parents are a specific thematic concern of *Queer as Folk 2*. In this respect, a key exchange occurs at Judith's wedding reception as Vince shares a pint with his father, Dudley. They are interrupted by a drunk Alexander, who introduces a new cocktail – 'Here, try that. It's brandy, gin and vodka. It's called a Jill Dando: one shot goes straight to your head' – and walks off. This one-liner, a near-the-knuckle camp gag at the expense of the murdered television presenter, generated fifteen

Vince, Dudley and Alexander at the wedding reception: Jill Dando

audience complaints to the television watchdog ITC, which were not
upheld. The ITC report on the 'joke' is revealing:

97

> Channel 4 ... explain[ed] that the sequel had set out to explore parent/
> child relationships, specifically focussing on fathers and sons. Alexander's
> father was dying and viewers were aware that this had been a difficult
> relationship. His reaction was to behave in an outrageous manner to
> disguise his vulnerable and damaged personality, eventually leading him to
> take an overdose. At the wedding, Alexander had difficulty coping with the
> cosy family sentiment and set out to get drunk. He deliberately interrupted
> Vince's tentative, but warm, conversation with his father with a remark that
> was shocking, outrageous and camp. It was not the intention that the
> audience should find this remark funny. Vince was mortified by the remark
> and his father embarrassed, with the conversation stopped in its tracks.
> When faced with this unpleasant and aggressively camp remark, Vince
> revealed a huge amount about his character. He rejected Dudley's offer of
> support and started lying about his status and relationship with Stuart,
> revealing a sense of shame about who he was.[85]

Indeed he does: after wincing at Alexander's lack of tact and sensitivity, Vince lies to his father that he and Stuart are an item, and that he has no money problems because Stuart is loaded.

The claim made by the ITC report that *Queer as Folk 2* examines relationships between parents and their offspring, particularly father/son connections, is true to some extent. What this statement ignores is that, as identified in Chapter 2, the role and significance of family – and 'queer family' – was examined at length in the original series. The quote also fudges the fact that fathers only feature in the sequel to a minor degree: Alexander's Dad is never seen, Roy Maloney has disappeared, Vince and Stuart's fathers do not figure in episode two. These limited appearances are significant in their own right, of course, especially in contrast to the marked amount of screen time taken up by Hazel and Janice: the relationships between gay men and their mothers are explored in depth in *Queer as Folk 2*, and seen as more important than bonds with fathers.

One significant distinction established by the first episode of the sequel is its depiction of Vince and Stuart's differing relationships with their respective Dads. At the wedding party, as Hazel and Stuart watch Vince chat to his father, Stuart caustically refers to the father and son as 'nodding dogs'. Vince and his Dad face each other, adopting similar seating positions, almost mirror images in their positioning. Vince lies to his father about his relationship with Stuart, and puffs up his own job status and self-esteem, but he is generous with his attention to his errant parent; Dudley, though clumsily and thoughtlessly homophobic, at least seems to care for his son, offering financial support and praising Vince's advances at Harlo's. Later in the episode, after Stuart's coming-out monologue, his father turns up at the Canal Street apartment. The two men are positioned at opposite sides of the frame, Stuart with his back to his father: there is an unbridgeable chasm between them. Stuart's father is attempting to make amends – he claims that his wife is 'trying to understand' her son's sexuality, to which Stuart snaps 'read a book' – but the absence of eye contact between the two men reveals Stuart's lack of interest in bonding with his Dad.

Dudley and Vince: nodding dogs

Stuart and his father

In contrast with these brief depictions of father/son dynamics, mothers play vital roles in *Queer as Folk 2*. The strength and resilience of Janice Maloney and Hazel Tyler are telegraphed in select scenes – in particular, in the kitchen table chat sequence in episode one. Janice becomes a regular presence on Canal Street. At Nathan's sixteenth birthday party in episode two, for instance, she is usually alongside him, spotted at one point dancing in an 'embarrassing Mum' fashion. Nathan is evidently somewhat humiliated by her presence, but her persistence and patience pay off: at the height of the party, the mother and son throw shapes together on the dancefloor. Following her memorable but

Janice and Hazel

100

Mrs Perry

often brief appearances in series one, Hazel develops significant depth as a character in *Queer as Folk 2*. Not only does she introduce or push forward specific narrative plotlines – including goading Stuart about his perverse relationship with Vince – but in the second episode she gets her hands dirty, securing Vince his promotion and engineering a high-speed dash by car across Manchester. In the realm of television drama, it is notable that a raft of gay male writers have, over the decades, created or shaped a host of strong, sparky and memorable female characters: Tony Warren's contributions to the first decade of *Coronation Street*, Darren Star's work on *Sex and the City* and Marc Cherry's for *Desperate Housewives* (Cherry Alley/Touchstone for ABC, 2004–) serve as obvious examples. Russell T. Davies's oeuvre as a whole can be seen to contribute to this history, another gay man writing feisty and absorbing female roles. The unique contribution of *Queer as Folk* is that, perhaps especially in its sequel, it takes on the stereotype about gay men having particularly intense relationships with their mothers, and provides the textured detail that enables audiences to comprehend how and why these bonds may form.

101

Unlike straight-talking, queer-friendly Hazel and sensitive, liberal Janice, Alexander's mother is portrayed as a monster. She is a bit of a shrew, beige cardigan worn over the shoulders, pinched mouth and black bob, 'not unlike a weasel wearing an Anna Wintour wig' according to Della Femina.[86] Mrs Perry is a rare figure in Russell T. Davies's writing: in series after series, he has created resilient, supportive, emotionally intelligent, likeable mothers, whose relationships with their children are often central to his plots and their dynamics. In the children's programme *Century Falls*, the main teenager, Tess Hunter (Catherine Sanderson), has moved to the eponymous rural village with her pregnant mother (Heather Baskerville, whose 'pregnancy' is indicated by her wearing a shapeless cream sweater throughout the series). Tess's mother is critical of her daughter – Tess is overweight, and given to flights of fancy – but the two also enjoy warm-hearted banter. In *Bob and Rose*, whose narrative follows a gay man falling in love with a woman, Bob's mother (Penelope Wilton), devoted to her son, has become a staunch advocate of gay rights. When Bob begins a romance with Rose, his relationship with his mother has to be carefully reworked and renegotiated. And in *Doctor Who*, Rose Tyler (Billie Piper) makes regular trips back home to London to see her mother, Jackie (Camille Coduri). Indeed, Jackie is a key character in the first two seasons of the relaunched science-fiction franchise, and although often placed in peril (killer Christmas trees, brainwashing by Cybermen), she has a working-class nous and an acid tongue that make her both entertaining and empathetic. Alexander's mother is nothing like any of these others: she is conservatively dressed, vindictive, lacking maternal sympathies. Indeed, the retributive violence that occurs against her in episode two is a serious judgment of her character.

Stuart's destruction of Mrs Perry's car enables *Queer as Folk 2* to engage with the ethics of direct-action political activism; it also allows the Stonewall/OutRage! tensions between Vince and Stuart to resurface. Although the jeep showroom incident in episode eight of the original series serves as an example of destructive political intervention, the sequel

'Bang': Mrs Perry's car is blown up

openly debates the morality and necessity of such actions through key exchanges between characters. Alexander, quietly cut up over his disinheritance, has taken an overdose. Stuart, furious at Alexander's parents, drives over to their suburban house, accompanied by Vince and baby Alfred. (A scene in which Stuart uses the internet to research how to make a bomb was shot, but cut from the final edit.) Mrs Perry's street is the epitome of the quiet English 'new build' estate of characterless houses, Brookside Close crossed with Hyacinth Bucket's residence in *Keeping Up Appearances* (BBC, 1990–5). In the middle of the street, Vince tries to talk Stuart out of doing anything rash. Their exchange once again brings to light the differing political attitudes of the two characters, Vince's non-interventionist stance contrasted with Stuart's radicalism (Stuart: 'Does she deserve it?'; Vince: 'You'll make it worse'). Vince walks away, in a shot that echoes the end of episode four of the first series, when he ran away from his mother's place, from Stuart's wanton recklessness and its repercussions. Stuart, acting alone, cuts the fuel line under Mrs Perry's car, petrol sloshing onto the tarmac. He knocks on her door: when she answers, he says 'bang', just as the car blows up behind him. In slow motion, against the backdrop of the burning vehicle, Stuart ambles backwards, grinning, his gangly movements an oddly syncopated dance of joyful spite. For the audience at home, the potential pleasures provided by this moment – both aesthetic and affective – need to be set against the extremism of Stuart's behaviour.

Later, at Nathan's party, Stuart's confrontation with Vince resumes:

> STUART: 'She deserved it.'
> VINCE: 'I know. But you tell her to fuck off. You always tell them to fuck off.'
> STUART: 'It's not enough any more.'
> VINCE: 'It is. You can't go and – There's people relying on me ... . I can't – You're on your own.'
> STUART: 'Suits me. You're just straight, Vince. You're a straight man who fucks men, that's all.'

This aggressive statement – which allies queer sexuality with specific political actions and behaviours, with a way of life that extends beyond the question of sexual preferences for one sex or another – knocks Vince, who walks away without responding. By the end of the episode, however, Vince becomes more like Stuart. Hazel (one of the 'people relying on' Vince financially) pushes him: she invades a briefing Vince is giving to the staff at Harlo's, and via a series of acetates and an overhead projector, goads him into joining Stuart, who is about to leave Manchester. After some hesitation, Vince tells slimy Graham to 'fuck off' and reveals the man's sexual infidelities to his fiancée, walks out of the supermarket and speeds with Hazel across Manchester, disrupting a marching group of child majorettes en route (a rather camp narrative embellishment). Stopped by the police, Hazel punches PC Des Stroud in the face, allowing Vince to run off to meet Stuart on Canal Street. Although Stuart initially resists Vince's desire to accompany him, he relents. The two now seem to be on a more equal footing: both are potentially in trouble with the police, both are ready to move on. Vince may not have committed a radical queer act of destruction, but he has uncovered a previously unseen reckless side to his personality – a behavioural trait that makes him more like Stuart. For his part, Stuart's departure is motivated by the recognition that Manchester's scene is small: he tells Romey as much; and an earlier brief moment shows him being laughed at by a group of younger men out on the scene, one of whom is Mickey. It may also be because he is getting older. Certainly, he is wound up about his age throughout *Queer as Folk 2*. Vince refers to him in jest as a 'wise old man', and Nathan asks him how many men he has left to have sex with. In Dantes, Stuart spots a man he fancies (actually Mark Ledsham, Mr Gay UK 1999), but is beaten to him by Nathan, a younger and arguably more appealing prospect. And in the intimate scene at the wedding when the audience is teased with the possibility that Vince and Stuart might finally have sex together, Vince reveals that Phil used to tell him that Stuart was saving Vince for his old age; Stuart replies: 'So the day I shag you, I'm old?'. All of these jibes make Stuart soften somewhat, and construct him as more sympathetic – and hence a little more like Vince.

Stuart and Vince's departure from Manchester is a notable set piece of the sequel. Nathan appears, his cocky strut down Canal Street not unlike Stuart's in the very first episode of the series. In a fairly lengthy speech whose delivery is accompanied by back-projection work, time-lapse cinematography and a dramatically escalating score, Vince and Stuart bequeath the city's scene and its wonders and horrors to the younger man. The duo run to the jeep and leap in. As a bright blue light glows from under the chassis, the vehicle smoothly rotates through 180 degrees. Suddenly, the jeep has special abilities, bringing to mind James Bond stunt vehicles, the Delorean in the *Back to the Future* film trilogy, Chitty Chitty Bang Bang, perhaps even the Tardis from *Doctor Who*: the step into science fiction highlights that this is now as much Vince's fantasy of escape as it is Stuart's. As Stuart speeds his fine four-fendered friend down Canal Street, the crowd scatter in a direct echo of the schoolchildren leaping out of the path of the jeep in episode one. Vince yells a final 'oh, my, God', the screen burns out white, and in a smooth cut the jeep reappears, somewhere over the rainbow, on an American highway which stretches into the horizon: the music segues into an upbeat 'hillbilly guitar' tune.

At a truckstop in Arizona (actually, these scenes were shot in Malaga), a passing hick calls Vince and Stuart 'faggots': Stuart pulls a weapon on the man, who apologises after some prompting from Vince. The pair have become outlaws, it would seem – a queer(er) version of *Thelma and Louise* (1991), perhaps. Or maybe *Bonnie and Clyde* (1967) is a more appropriate comparison point: the sequel's end credits reveal final narrative trajectories for the series' main characters, concluding with the comment that 'There are many rumours about Stuart and Vince, all of them true', which imbues the pair with the status of legends. The Arizona sequence in fact calls to mind American New Queer Cinema films of the early 1990s in which gay male couples took to the highway, such as *My Own Private Idaho* (1991) or *The Living End* (1992). The first shot of Vince and Stuart's jeep on the US highway even seems to be a direct quote of an image from *Idaho* – of the road that Mike (River Phoenix) says looks like a 'fucked-up face'.

The jeep becomes a magic car

The jeep in Arizona

The 'fucked-up face' in *My Own Private Idaho*

These final minutes of *Queer as Folk 2* – the science-fiction jeep with its 'hyperdrive' leap to a different country, the buddy/road-movie confrontation in the US – invite audiences to retrospectively consider the generic status of the programme. Some reviewers of the first series noted its shifting textures. Alkarim Jivani, for instance, identified its 'ability to strike a tone which touched on several different genres so that the series played like a cross between *Soap!*, *thirtysomething* and *Lancashire Loveboys – Hard and Hung*'.[87] This generic hybridity, especially notable in the final instalment of the sequel, is playfully post-modern, enabling connections to be made to other drama series of the 1980s and 1990s such as *The Singing Detective* (ABC/BBC, 1986) and *Twin Peaks* (Lynch and Frost/Spelling for ABC, 1990–1) which blurred the lines between known forms of storytelling. But as a queer drama, it also opens up space for comparison with other instances of queer artists appropriating (and meddling with, or paying tribute to) mainstream genres, from George Kuchar's lo-fi fake melodramas to Andy Warhol's 'Western' *Lonesome Cowboys* (1969), from Su Friedrich's nun movie *Damed If You Don't* (1987) to Todd Haynes's *Far from Heaven* (2002). And there is a clear connection to New Queer Cinema, for B. Ruby Rich identified the dominant aesthetic of the film movement as 'Homo Pomo': science-fiction elements also suddenly appear, for instance, in Gregg Araki's teen film *Nowhere*.

107

Despite the finality of the ending of *Queer as Folk 2*, and Russell T. Davies's satisfaction in being allowed to cut down the sequel from ten hours to two, the series – and the characters – refused to die. At one point in 2000, Channel 4 was planning to develop its own gay website. Davies began putting together short stories, mini-episodes, featuring the *Queer as Folk* characters for the website, but it never materialised. More importantly, Channel 4 also asked Davies to develop a spin-off series from *Queer as Folk*. Entitled *Misfits* – although at one point it was known as *Hazel's House* – the programme would have placed Hazel and her tenants (Bernie, Alexander, maybe Donna) centre-stage. In an interview with the website *Television without Pity*, Davies highlighted that the spin-off would not have been 'one hundred percent gay – that's why it was called *Misfits*, a bunch of people who don't fit in anywhere; that notion of the inverted, extended family'.[88] He also detailed the planned plot of the show:

> Hazel marrying the lovely PC, Des Stroud, was the backbone of the entire series. Cos it was a marriage just doomed to failure; though he's a lovely bloke, and loves Hazel completely, she actually marries him for a bit of financial stability – Vince really did keep that house afloat – and, more importantly, because she's bereft, practically in mourning. Her son – the man she's spent 30 years with, seeing him practically every day – ups and disappears, and she's left with no one. And there's Des. His story was fab, too – a good, law-abiding man, thrown into this world of misfits, and actually loving it. So the series started three episodes before the wedding, and then charted the gradual decline of two lovely, well-meaning people who've trapped themselves. [. . .] Craig Kelly had agreed to come back for the first four episodes, to marry off his mum, and Charlie had potentially agreed to come back for the wedding episode.[89]

108

Shaking off the world of *Queer as Folk* was harder than initially thought, it would seem:

> For all my reservations, I had plenty more things to say. I can't help it – I think of stories all the time, that's why I'm in this job. And there were plenty of brilliant writers that Nicola and I wanted to work with, to share the workload. So we developed a 20-episode series, and I swear the first two episodes are the best thing I've ever written, and Channel 4 loved it … And then said no. Maybe time and tastes had moved on. I don't know, because we never had a proper explanation. In fact, we had no explanation at all.[90]

The relationship between Davies and Channel 4 started to sour. They also pulled the plug on *The Second Coming*, a drama about the son of God returning to Earth (Manchester, in fact). He worked on the script for ten months, writing a four-hour programme, and then 'did about fifteen rewrites to everyone's satisfaction'.[91] The project was greenlit, and then cancelled: *The Second Coming* was eventually supported and screened by ITV. The treatment of these three projects – the short web stories, *Misfits*, *The Second Coming* – evidently caused Davies serious grief. In an interview with gay.com conducted in November 2000, he discussed candidly his treatment by Channel 4, the time and money wasted, and his reticence at ever working for the channel again.[92] And, indeed, Davies has subsequently avoided Channel 4: everything he has developed and written since *Queer as Folk* has been produced either for Carlton/ITV or for the BBC.

4 Gay as Blazes

Although the production story of the British version of *Queer as Folk* concluded rather acrimoniously, with Russell T. Davies falling out with Channel 4, the tale of the series does not end there. In October 1999, the *Guardian* announced that *Queer as Folk* was to be remade for an American audience.[93] Gub Neal signed a deal with the William Morris agency and sold three British dramas to American television companies: *Queer as Folk*, *The Young Person's Guide to Being a Rock Star* and *Love in the 21st Century* (the latter, incidentally, also a Red Productions series). Initially, renowned Hollywood figure Joel Schumacher was attached to the remake of *Queer as Folk*. An openly gay director, Schumacher had queer credentials: he had written the script for *Car Wash* (1976), directed two campy instalments of the Batman franchise, and made the drag-queen drama *Flawless* (1999). He planned to re-locate the narratives and characters of *Queer as Folk* to New Jersey, and predicted that the new version of the series would be as controversial in the US as the original had been in the UK: 'I like to stir things up a little. Whenever I see fundamentalist Christians hooting it up on TV, I think "Wait till they get a load of this".'[94] At one point, Rob Dwek, a former executive for primetime programming at Fox, was engaged as a consultant for the pilot episode of the remake: Dwek and Neal had previously worked together on the US translation of *Cracker*.[95]

The American version of *Queer as Folk* was pitched by Channel 4 to cable channel HBO but, according to Kristin Hohenadel, 'HBO dropped out after a sticking point on format – whether it was more suited to a series or a movie, with Channel Four wanting the former, HBO the latter.'[96] After further behind-the-scenes machinations – including the departure of Schumacher, who had to leave to make a film – *Queer as Folk US* (as it is usually known, to distinguish it from the original) went into manufacture as a joint American–Canadian venture. Assembled by CowLip Productions, Tony Jonas Productions and Temple Street Productions in association with Channel 4 Television and Showcase Television, the series was broadcast on cable channel Showtime in America (whose slogan is 'No Limits') and on commercial network Showcase in Canada. Ultimately, *Queer as Folk US* ran for five seasons (2000–5), lasting for a total of eighty-three episodes: seasons three to five were somewhat shorter than the first two. It was developed for television by Ron Cowen and Daniel Lipman, who remained the series' main storyliners throughout its five-season run. Cowen and Lipman – real-life partners, as well as business associates – had previously worked as writers and associate producers on *An Early Frost*, the Emmy Award-winning 1985 NBC television drama about AIDS, and as the creators and executive producers of the series *Sisters* (CowLip/Lorimar/WB for NBC, 1991–6). Russell T. Davies actually had very little to do with the remake of *Queer as Folk*. In a 2002 interview, he said that his input had involved a

111

> couple of nice meetings, lots of phone calls at the beginning just chatting about it, and now it's like one phone call a month and one email a month. And they flew me over there once but that was just like for publicity purposes, it was like when they launched it, it was good for them to have my seal of approval. Certainly, you know, in terms of gay press … . But I just let them get on with it.[97]

In a book of this size, it is impossible to do justice to the size, scope, content, feel and highs and lows of the US version of *Queer as Folk*, which – especially from season two onwards – is a markedly different programme to the original. In this brief concluding chapter, I merely wish to make some observations on the remake: how the British material was reshaped for consumption on the other side of the Atlantic; alterations that were made, as well as aspects that were retained; decisions about casting, setting, direction and so on that contributed to *Queer as Folk US*'s distinctive tenor and grain; the ways in which the series handled matters of sex and politics. There is enough material in the remake's eighty-three episodes to warrant a separate book-length study: what appears here is merely an introduction, a comparison, some preliminary thoughts and discussion.

Queer as Folk US relocated the stories and characters from the original series to Pittsburgh: allegedly chosen as an appropriate stand-in for Manchester, Pittsburgh's greatest queer claim to fame is that it boasts the Andy Warhol Museum. Despite adopting this location, the series was shot in Canada due to tax incentives. A significant amount of the programme was made in or near Toronto: the series was shot largely at Dufferin Gate Studios in Etobicoke, Ontario, with significant amounts of location filming conducted in Toronto's Church and Wellesley gay district. (An episode in season four in which the main characters visit Toronto contains a number of gags in which individuals point out how much Toronto looks like Pittsburgh.) Although individual episodes were attributed to specific scriptwriters, like many American drama series *Queer as Folk US* was fundamentally written by committee: group storylining meetings were followed by an allocation of instalments to specific writers, but their ideas and outlines would be brought back to the committee for approval. Episodes of the remade version throughout its five seasons were often directed by individuals associated with Canadian independent cinema, including Jeremy Podeswa and John Greyson; several episodes of the first season were helmed by the Australian Russell Mulcahy, best known as a director of pop promos.

Despite the change in setting, character templates and specific locations remained largely similar to the original. Brian Kinney is Stuart's equivalent: he has a job in advertising and owns a spacious loft apartment, modelled closely on Stuart's abode. Michael Novotny is the US version of Vince, who – initially, at least – works in a supermarket

Michael and Brian on the hospital roof

called The Big Q. Rather than being a fan of science fiction, Michael is a comic-book geek, devoted to a character called Captain Astro. (In the pilot episode of the first season, when Michael and Brian have escaped to the roof of the hospital in which Brian's son Gus has just been born, rather than recreate an iconic scene from *Titanic* the two men have a Superman/Lois Lane moment.) Justin Taylor is a seventeen-year-old rendering of Nathan, those two additional years a clear indication of the US need to be more sensitive about the age-of-consent issue. Alexander Perry becomes the flaming Emmett Honeycutt who works in a fashion boutique called Torso and Phil Delaney is accountant Ted Schmidt; Romey and Lisa become, respectively, art teacher and gallery assistant Lindsay Peterson and lawyer Melanie Marcus. In a casting coup – especially taking into account Alexander's gag in episode seven of the original series, 'I'm Christine Cagney and I'm an alcoholic' – Michael's mother, Debbie Novotny, is played by Sharon Gless, Cagney of *Cagney and Lacey* (Orion/CBS, 1982–8). Debbie waits tables at the Liberty Diner on Liberty Avenue, the main drag of Pittsburgh's gay

Debbie Novotny

village: she is most often depicted wearing a slogan T-shirt ('You say tomato, I say fuck off', 'Just because I'm a Mom doesn't mean I care', and so on), a red wig, and a rainbow-coloured waistcoat covered with gay rights badges. *Queer as Folk US* is in fact heavily invested in the rainbow flag as a symbol of queer community: even the title of the series, as it appears in the opening credits of the programme, is underlined by a rainbow stripe. This symbol has been associated with lesbian and gay culture since the 1970s: it is recognised internationally and marks queer venues in many a city. However, it is also ruthlessly exploited by the makers of queer consumer goods, such that lesbian/gay stores often overflow with rainbow-themed merchandise. Episodes of the sitcoms *Will and Grace* and *Ellen* have satirised the mercenary milking of this symbol. In an episode of her sitcom, for instance, shortly after coming out, Ellen was given a rainbow air freshener by one of her friends; sniffing it, she claimed that it 'smelled gay'. The po-faced adoption of the rainbow flag in *Queer as Folk US* ties the series to mainstream commercial gay culture, to the widespread dissemination of a specific version of queer life, in a more overt manner than the original series did.

114

This connection to a dominant market-driven financially lucrative lesbian/gay culture can also be witnessed in *Queer as Folk US* in its use of the gym as a key location, and in its focus on the type of muscular bodies produced by gym training. The characters in the UK series never visit the gym and are never shown exercising. The body type that the series favours is thin but toned: Gillen's lithe athletic frame is routinely exposed and Hunnam's taut torso is notably lingered on in episode four. In fact, it could be argued that the British series foregrounds, in terms of its representations of men's bodies, a twink aesthetic – the term 'twink' used in gay circles to refer to young, youthful, pretty but skinny boys. In contrast, all of the male characters in the US version regularly work out, and some (most notably Ben, a regular character in series two to five, and Drew, who appears in the last two seasons) are significantly pumped up. The scenes set in the nightclub Babylon (this name adopted from the UK version) usually begin with cameras tracing through the space, capturing buffed go-go boys in minimal clothing dancing on podia. The hairless, sculpted torso is not

115

Babylon, in *Queer as Folk US*

only the predominant physical type depicted in the series – it is also the one preferred and disseminated by the mainstream US magazines pitched at a wealthy urban demographic (*The Advocate*, *Genre*), and by advertisers attempting to capture the attention of the same audience. This aspect of *Queer as Folk US*, which evidently may operate as a source of considerable visual pleasure for some viewers, thus reflects the manufactured tastes of a mainstreamed gay identity.

The first season of *Queer as Folk US* lasted for twenty-two episodes. It was advertised with a widespread campaign that cost more than 10 million dollars, and that included billboard posters, promotional parties in gay venues, free merchandise (postcards, coasters), direct-mail brochures and internet site banners. Across the run of this season, the character development and dense plot of the first British series were stretched out, attenuated: material that filled up around four and a half hours on British television became about twenty hours of screen time. (In fact, I am tempted to compare this first American season – and its British source – to Douglas Gordon's art installation *24 Hour Psycho*, which slowed down Hitchcock's 1960 film so that it took twenty-four hours to unspool, enabling spectators to contemplate every single frame of the film.) Although new elements were introduced, especially for the characters that were more minor – or actually written out – in the initial British series, audiences familiar with the original would experience déjà vu at the level of narrative incident. A great deal remains in place: though the 'unrequited love' aspect of their bond is played down, Michael is devoted to Brian; Michael has a relationship with an older, more sensible man – a chiropractor known as Dr David – but leaves him at the end of the season to return to his friends; Justin masturbates homophobic bully Chris Hobbs (the only character name retained from the UK original) in the gym changing rooms at school; Lindsay plans to marry an immigrant called Guillaume to enable him to stay in the country; and so on. Even the title 'Queer as Folk' remained, despite its quintessential Englishness: American reviews and articles about the series – the original or the remake – regularly contained a clause explaining to readers exactly what the phrase meant.

Queer as Folk US credits series 1–3

Queer as Folk US credits series 4–5

And yet in many ways this first season is also a notably distinct creature. In contrast to the ambiguous credits of the UK series, the US opening titles are loud and gaudy. Greek Buck's frenetic track 'Spunk' plays over spinning patterns of lurid colours, and a succession of athletic boys in underwear posture and dance, or swim in front of the camera.

The letters of the word 'queer' spin, 3D, towards the camera in succession. These credits seem hedonistic and are explicitly focused on male bodies: they seem to directly reference the visual and haptic pleasures of the gay club scene. (The credits of seasons four and five are different: a little less frantic, set to a different song and shot largely in black and white, they depict the main cast members in iconic moments of interaction – hugging, dancing, laughing, kissing – as well as gyrating models, some of whom wear queer issues slogan T-shirts.) There are new plot strands that add to character development. Ted – just like Phil in the original – overdoses on drugs after picking up a man called Blake. Although briefly put into a coma, he recovers, and throughout the five seasons of *Queer as Folk US* Ted and Blake have a complicated on-off relationship. Brian fucks a subordinate at work and finds himself slapped with a sexual harassment suit, which Justin helps him to escape. Emmett joins a conversion-therapy course and attempts (disastrously) to 'go straight'. The lesbian couple, Melanie and Lindsay, are afforded much more screen time: although most of their plots revolve around domestic arrangements, parenting and sex, their characters are substantially fleshed out. And in the season finale, Justin takes Brian to his high-school prom, but Chris Hobbs attacks his fellow student with a baseball bat, landing Justin in hospital.

The pilot episode of *Queer as Folk US* was directed by Russell Mulcahy, and some of the stylistic tropes that he adopted remained in place for the five seasons of the show. Although for more intimate moments of conversation, especially in domestic contexts, the camera remains still, on the whole Mulcahy's directorial signature involves mobile camera work, dynamic zooming and panning, and a swift editing pace. Two specific strategies stand out as distinctive, both of which are used to offer some insight into character subjectivity and emotion. First, camera speed often alters within a shot, integrating short bursts of speeded-up or slowed-down footage. Second, a zoom or a speeded-up moment will often climax with a small 'explosion': the frame will lighten a little, and a subdued 'boom' will be heard on the soundtrack. As with the British series, music is used throughout the remake (around

250 different songs were used in the first season alone), and some of the choices made comment literally on the action depicted. For instance, in a slight variation from the original programme, when Brian first snogs Justin in his apartment the song that accompanies them is Divine's disco track 'You Think You're a Man' ('but you're only a boy'); the same song was used in the British version to accompany Nathan's maiden visit to a gay bar.

A major distinction between the UK and US versions of *Queer as Folk* is the number and frequency of sex scenes. Showtime, as a cable channel, offers to its subscribers aspects of representation that the commercial networks have to avoid in order to appease advertisers and appeal to the largest possible audience. In other words, American audiences of *Queer as Folk US* – as with those who subscribed to HBO to watch series such as *Oz* (Levinson and Fontana/Rysher, 1997–2003), *Sex and the City* and *The Sopranos* (Chase Films/Brad Grey, 1999–2007) – would have expected elements such as nudity, sex and swearing. Almost every episode of the US remake contains at least one sex scene, many of which are anatomically unbelievable. Although sometimes these are included for humorous reasons (there is a rapid montage in one episode when Emmett, supposedly interviewing potential new flatmates, is fucked by each candidate), the coitus often seems to be incorporated to satisfy the audience desire to see queer sex on television. Unlike the few short scenes of fornication in the UK original, which were almost all designed to reveal elements of story, the fucking in *Queer as Folk US* serves different purposes. Executive producer Daniel Lipman claimed that they offer an insight into character psychology:

119

> What we've learned is that showing sex is very much like opera ...
> In opera, the reason people sing and go into their aria is because language can only take you so far in terms of expressing emotion. When you sing, it's expansive and that's how you express your emotion. It's the same thing with sex. We have sex for many reasons, whether it's anger, vengeance, joy, celebration, or despair.[98]

Notably, the sheer volume of sex scenes in *Queer as Folk US* produces a significantly more diverse and complex picture of human sexuality than the small number of (mostly vanilla) sequences in the original. Dildos, sadomasochism, foursomes, bathhouse orgies and fetishism all feature alongside a range of other practices. Lesbian characters have sex with men; gay male leads (Justin, Emmett) have sex with women (if rather reluctantly). Thus, a much more broadly 'queer' conception of non-normative sexual activity is put forward, with experimentation and identity malleability regularly foregrounded.

Queer as Folk US, like the UK original, succeeded in filling a representational void, and for this it was praised by audiences and critics. Joyce Millman called the show 'the first American series (sorry, *Ellen*) to capture gay life in all its glorious complexity, without preachiness, polemics or self-censorship'.[99] And Walter Chaw praised the programme's 'audacity', writing that 'it's instantly clear that *Queer as Folk* is groundbreaking in what it dares to show (almost no peculiarity of homosexual intercourse is left mysterious) and courageous

120

Sex in *Queer as Folk US*

in light of the open hostility still displayed toward homosexuals in the shockingly prudish United States'.[100] The show drew high ratings for Showtime and Showcase, swiftly establishing itself as Showtime's most successful programme. The appeal of the series was international: the US version of *Queer as Folk* has been successfully exported to a host of other countries, including Brazil, Hungary, Slovenia, Germany, Spain and Australia. In the UK, the BBC bought the screening rights to seasons one and two: the first was shown on the digital channel BBC Choice, but the second was never aired. Seasons three and four were bought by Channel 4 and screened on their offshoot E4 (albeit without advertising of any form, in a graveyard slot). As late as 2006, a poll in *The Advocate* identified *Queer as Folk US* as a significantly important aspect of American readers' 'personal LGBT experience': the series was ranked markedly higher than Madonna or Cher.[101] However, like the original programme, the remake also had its detractors: the series was criticised for its focus on white characters, for its lack of realism, for its (stereotypical) focus on sex. In this regard, it is worth noting that *Queer as Folk US* featured a disclaimer after every episode when it aired on Showtime: '*Queer as Folk* is a celebration of the lives and passions of a group of gay friends. It is not meant to reflect all of gay society.'

121

Arguably, it was only with the second season that *Queer as Folk US* began to break free of its roots in the original British series. Although fragments of the UK version occasionally cropped up, the US series from this point took off on its own. The plotlines introduced became considerably more soap-like: there were drug addictions, deaths, weddings, a pregnancy, arrests, ill-advised couplings, counselling sessions, legal battles, adoption attempts, bomb attacks, financial crises, life-threatening illnesses and surgery, falling-outs and making-ups. For much of its run, the series adopted a standard narrative form: the typical episode of *Queer as Folk US* opened in Babylon, then moved to a scene set at the diner; three narrative strands would be introduced and spun out, all of which would come to a relatively neat conclusion by the end of the episode, in a scene set back in the club. There were diversions from, and alterations to, this formula – season four's episodes, for instance, were a little longer and therefore featured more story strands – but the template was adhered to fairly rigidly.

Within this narrative structure, the series' creators explored a raft of queer political issues much more overtly than in the original British series. The characters attend a pride rally; they help out an ailing HIV-support centre by taking part in a sponsored bike ride; in the final season, they work to prevent the introduction of a piece of anti-gay legislation called Proposition 14, handing out leaflets, canvassing and displaying banners. In season three, Brian works for a conservative mayoral candidate called Stockwell, directing his advertising campaign. But Stockwell is helping to close down – or 'clean up' – queer venues on Liberty Avenue, in an echo of Rudy Giuliani's efforts to Disneyfy Times Square in New York. Brian bankrolls a campaign against Stockwell: he bankrupts himself, but succeeds in causing the politician's downfall. Some of the topics depicted and explored in *Queer as Folk US* also appeared in the original series: same-sex parenting; homophobia at school and in the workplace; recreational drug use; vigilantism (in season four, Justin joins a direct-action group called the Pink Posse). But there are countless others: the politics of barebacking (unprotected anal sex), the existence of 'bugchasers' (individuals who want to be infected with HIV), marriage and adoption rights, prostitution, gay men in the clergy, the film industry's homophobia and its closeting of actors … . Throughout, most of the characters advocate a community-centred sensibility. Discussing requests for donations to gay charity events in the first episode of season four, for instance, Emmett asks rhetorically 'If we don't help ourselves, who else will?'. And Ben (a professor of lesbian and gay studies, no less) is often encumbered with leaden dialogue about the political significance of gay support networks and venues. Only Brian, like Stuart in the original series, routinely voices an alternative dissenting perspective – but even he steps in financially when the scene which provides him with regular no-strings-attached sex is threatened.

In addition to the political issues already mentioned, *Queer as Folk US* also self-reflexively examined its own contribution to ongoing debates about queer representation in the mass media. Series two

Gay as Blazes

introduced a show-within-the-show called *Gay as Blazes*. Hysterically
PC, *Gay as Blazes* features a multi-ethnic cast, one of whom is in a
wheelchair. The characters sing the virtues of monogamy and fidelity,
and damn a friend who can't keep away from 'Club Sodom': 'Hopefully
one day he'll come to his senses and realize that his time could be spent
in so many more productive ways, like joining a gay men's reading
group.' The irony is that, by the end of its fifth season, almost all of the
main characters in *Queer as Folk US* were settled in monogamous
couples, having children, and abandoning the bar and club scene by
moving to the suburbs. In an additional interrogation of television's
depictions of queer lives, the final season of the remake featured a
plotline in which Emmett was given a slot on a local news bulletin as
their 'queer guy', dispensing tips about fashion, style and etiquette –
a clear reference to the reality makeover series *Queer Eye for the Straight
Guy*. Emmett was told by station bosses that he could only keep this
position if he didn't talk about sex; his homosexuality had to be sanitised
and safe. Anna McCarthy has levelled a similar criticism against *Queer*

Eye, noting of its presenters that '[t]he Fab Five are totally sexless. They may tease their subjects, but there is no chance that they will get to sleep with them.'[102] Thus, when Emmett kissed his boyfriend Drew in front of the camera his television career was brought to a swift end.

Picking up on the potential of the UK original, perhaps the most significant contribution that *Queer as Folk US* made to 'gay television' was that it definitively proved that the lives of lesbians and gay men could be narrativised, formatted into an episodic structure – and that this would reach a regular, appreciative audience. The self-contained world of *Queer as Folk US* – and there are hardly any heterosexual characters in the show, besides Debbie – provided enough stories and incidents to sustain five seasons' worth of programming. Admittedly, the remake was at times rather sluggish and tedious: as Jacques Peretti noted of the first American season, 'Sexier than one had imagined American advertisers allowing, US *Queer as Folk* is nevertheless dull. It's as slick and humourless as a soft porn video, and as boring as watching *Newsnight* without Jeremy Paxman.'[103] And yet this critic's experience of boredom could in itself be recuperated as having political significance. Queer people and fictional characters are usually assumed to be interesting and engaging as a result of their liminal positioning, their marginality. But most lesbians and gay men lead lives that are frequently as humdrum and ordinary as those of heterosexuals: depicting this in an ongoing soap-like format was in itself a fresh strategy, if one that tends to reinforce the assimilationist perspective that 'we are just like you'.

* * *

Abstract blurred lights, shot through a coloured filter, drift slowly across the screen, accompanied by an upbeat melodic xylophone score by Murray Gold. As the drama starts, revellers exit busy Manchester bars, one gay reveller heading off for a sexual encounter that is brought to an unexpectedly swift and comedic end. This isn't *Queer as Folk*, but *Bob and Rose*, Russell T. Davies's first major drama after his year of projects falling through with Channel 4. The six-part series, which starred Alan Davies as Bob and Lesley Sharp as Rose, told another queer story of love and relationships in Manchester, this time focusing on a romance between a gay man and a straight woman. Russell T. Davies has called *Bob and Rose*

> the gayest thing I've ever written. Because over six weeks, everyone comes out of the closet – unloved wives, secret James Bond fans, and those who are simply lonely, all harbouring some sort of love that dares not speak its name. And all realising, through the actions of Bob and Rose, that they can shout it out loud.[104]

In his subsequent work, Davies has continued to include queer characters. There is another gay teenager – like Nathan Maloney, also fifteen years old – in *Mine All Mine*. Casanova (David Tennant), in Davies's version of the tale, falls for a beautiful castrato called Bellino, only to discover that 'he' is really a woman (played by Nina Sosanya). And with *Doctor Who* and its subsequent spin-off, *Torchwood* (CBC/BBC, 2006–), Davies introduced the character of Captain Jack, a pansexual time-traveller from the 51st century (John Barrowman). In an interview that appeared to promote the start of *Torchwood*, Davies commented that:

> This is the next stage of my plan to make everyone on TV gay ...
> Without making it political and dull, this is going to be a very bisexual programme ... I want to knock down the barriers so we can't define which of the characters is gay. We need to start mixing things up, rather than saying, 'This is a gay character and he'll only ever go off with men'.[105]

Certainly, Davies's contributions to 'gay television' over the last decade – since the appearance of Clive the barman, in fact – have been considerable. *Queer as Folk* worked as Davies's calling card, and his status within the industry has only improved since: not only was he awarded the Dennis Potter Award for Outstanding Writing for Television at the 2006 BAFTAs, but he is (at the time of writing) steering three separate strands of the reinvigorated *Doctor Who* franchise:

125

the original series, adult-oriented *Torchwood* and the children's programme *The Sarah Jane Adventures* (BBC, 2007–).

As mentioned in the introduction to this book, *Queer as Folk* not only kickstarted Davies's career, but also that of Red Productions. Shindler's company followed up *Queer as Folk* with, among others, *Clocking Off*, *Linda Green*, *Bob and Rose* and *Conviction* (2004). As for the three directors of the series, Charles McDougall has helmed episodes of *Sex and the City*, *Desperate Housewives* and the US remake of *The Office* (Reveille/NBC, 2005–), Sarah Harding has continued to work in British television and Menhaj Huda directed the film *Kidulthood* (2006).

Tipping the Velvet

Noah's Arc

Of the cast, Antony Cotton secured a regular role in *Coronation Street*, and Aidan Gillen has featured in the critically acclaimed US series *The Wire* (Blown Deadline Productions for HBO, 2002–). Charlie Hunnam has arguably had the most successful career post-*Queer as Folk*: after appearing in the cancelled US teen series *Young Americans* (Columbia Tristar/Mandalay for WB, 2000) and *Undeclared* (Apatow Productions/Dreamworks for Fox, 2001–2) and doing some modelling work, he has had prominent roles in the films *Nicholas Nickleby* (2002), *Green Street* (2005) and *Children of Men* (2006).

   In the wake of *Queer as Folk*, only a small number of television series focusing almost exclusively on queer characters have appeared, and these have been of varying quality and success. In the UK, these include: *Metrosexuality* (1999), written by Rikki Beadle-Blair and centred mostly on non-white characters; two adaptations of Sarah Waters' Victoriana novels, *Tipping the Velvet* (BBC, 2002) and *Fingersmith* (BBC, 2005); and, arguably, *The Line of Beauty* (BBC, 2006), adapted by Andrew Davies from Alan Hollinghurst's book. Queer characters were also placed centre-stage in *The Long Firm* (BBC, 2004), a screen version of Jake Arnott's gangster novel, and *Sugar Rush*

(Shine for Channel 4, 2005–), a cheap and cheerful Brighton-set lesbian schoolgirl drama, based on the book of the same name by Julie Burchill. In the US, Showtime followed up their version of *Queer as Folk* with dyke drama *The L Word* (Anonymous Content/Dufferin Gate/Viacom, 2004–), just entering its fourth season, and NBC's *Will and Grace* attained substantial success, running for eight seasons. Programmes have been produced for channels niche-targeted at the queer market: Los Angeles-set black gay drama *Noah's Arc* on Logo (Open Door/Blueprint, 2005–), and supernatural-themed *Dante's Cove* (A.C.H. GmbH/Regent Entertainment, 2005–; tagline: 'Possessed and Undressed') on Here! TV. All indebted in some sense to the inroads made by *Queer as Folk*, in terms of what would be accepted by television producers and audiences, these subsequent programmes have, in their own ways, continued the battles for complex forms of queer representation fought by Davies's series. For, despite claims from journalists, academics and other commentators that social and political attitudes towards non-straight sexualities have relaxed somewhat in the last decade, getting queer characters and stories on television remains a difficult, complicated and politically fraught task. In retrospect, what *Queer as Folk* was able to accomplish seems almost miraculous.

128

Notes

1 Rob Brown (2001), 'I Never Saw *Queer as Folk* as a Gay Drama', *Guardian*, 9 April.
2 Stuart Millar and Janine Gibson (1999), 'Channel 4 Glad to Pioneer the First Gay Drama on British TV', *Guardian*, 24 February, p. 3; Pegg is quoted in Millar and Gibson's article.
3 Megan Radclyffe (1999), 'This Queer Life', *Gay Times* no. 246, March, p. 7.
4 Alkarim Jivani (1999), preview of *Queer as Folk*, *Time Out* no. 1488, 24 February – 3 March, pp. 186–7; Rupert Smith (2000), 'Men Behaving Madly', *Guardian*, 16 February.
5 Mark Lawson (2004), 'Lawson on TV', *Guardian*, 5 January.
6 Nicola Shindler quoted in Brown (2001), 'I Never Saw *Queer as Folk* as a Gay Drama'.
7 See, for instance, comments made by some of the contributors to the two-part *The South Bank Show: TV Drama Stories* documentary screened on ITV in February 2004.
8 Jeremy Isaacs, the fiirst chief executive of Channel 4, discusses the controversy aroused by the Jarman screenings in his 1989 book *Storm over 4: A Personal Account* (London: Weidenfeld and Nicolson), pp. 120–2. For a detailed analysis of *Out on Tuesday* and *Out*, see Colin Richardson (1995), 'TVOD: The Never-Bending Story', in Paul Burston and Colin Richardson (eds), *A Queer Romance: Lesbians, Gay Men and Popular Culture* (London and New York: Routledge), pp. 216–48.
9 Chris Higgins (1999), 'Folk Like Us', *Gay Times* no. 244, January, p. 19.
10 Quoted in Millar and Gibson (1999), 'Channel 4 Glad to Pioneer the First Gay Drama on British TV', p. 3.
11 See, for instance, Simon Fanshawe (1998), 'The Age of Consent', *Guardian*, Saturday review, 7 November, pp. 1–2, which was illustrated with an image of Charlie Hunnam before the fiirst episode of *Queer as Folk* had even aired.
12 Duncan Marr (2000), 'Spunk on the Screen', *Gay Times* no. 257, February, p. 17.
13 Andy Medhurst (1994), 'One Queen and His Screen: Lesbian and Gay Television', in Emma Healey and Angela Mason (eds), *Stonewall 25: The Making of the Lesbian and Gay Community in Britain* (London: Virago), p. 239.
14 Ibid.
15 Rupert Smith (2006), 'That Crucial Broadcast: *The Naked Civil Servant*', *Gay Times* no. 337, October, p. 19.
16 Alan McKee (2002), 'Interview with Russell T. Davies', *Continuum: Journal of Media and Cultural Studies* vol. 16 no. 2, p. 237.
17 Russell T. Davies (2003), *Queer as Folk: Defiinitive Collector's Edition* DVD booklet, pp. 7–9.
18 McKee, 'Interview with Russell T. Davies', p. 238.
19 Davies, *Queer as Folk* DVD booklet, p. 10.
20 According to Peter Billingham (2005), 'audience research revealed that the series' largest single demographic viewing group was made up of young women between the ages of eighteen and thirty'. 'Can Kinky Sex Ever Be Politically Correct? *Queer as Folk* and the Geo-ideological Inscription of Gay Sexuality', in Jonathan Bignell and Stephen Lacey (eds), *Popular Television Drama: Critical Perspectives* (Manchester: Manchester University Press), p. 122.
21 Quoted in Anon (1999), 'Sparks Fly over *Queer as Folk*', *Pink Paper* no. 573, 5 March.
22 Quoted in Terry Sanderson (1999), 'There's Nowt So Queer as Hacks', *Gay Times* no. 247, April, p. 67.
23 David Smith (1999), Letters page, *Time Out* no. 1489, 3–10 March, p. 202.
24 Quoted in Sarah Lyall (1999), 'Three Gay Guys on British TV: What's the Fuss?', *New York Times*, 15 April.
25 Russell T. Davies (1999), 'Queer as Fuck', *Attitude*, June, p. 34.
26 Marr, 'Spunk on the Screen', p. 18.
27 Medhurst, 'One Queen and His Screen', p. 243.
28 Quoted in Lyall, 'Three Gay Guys on British TV'.
29 B. Ruby Rich (1992), 'New Queer Cinema', *Sight and Sound* vol. 2 no. 5, September, pp. 30–5; see also Michele Aaron (ed.) (2004), *New Queer Cinema: A Critical Reader*

(Edinburgh: Edinburgh University Press). For more information on queercore – also sometimes known as homocore – see David Ciminelli and Ken Knox (2005), *Homocore: The Loud and Raucous Rise of Queer Rock* (New York: Alyson).

30 See, for instance, Garry Maddox (2004), 'Is *Sex and the City* Gay?', *Sydney Morning Herald*, 9 February. As Maddox noted, 'Even Marge Simpson has recognised the secret to *Sex and the City*. "That's the show about four women acting like gay guys", she said in a recent episode of *The Simpsons*.'

31 Anon, 'Sparks Fly over *Queer as Folk*'.

32 Colin Richardson (1999), 'Sponsors Fight Shy of Gay TV', *Gay Times* no. 248, May, p. 53.

33 Janine Gibson (1999), 'Gay Programme Upsets Viewers', *Guardian*, 22 June, p. 5.

34 See Duncan Marr (1999), 'Queer as Folk – The Verdict', *Gay Times* no. 248, May, p. 94.

35 McKee, 'Interview with Russell T. Davies', p. 236.

36 Nicola Shindler, interview in 'Making of' documentary 'What the Folk?', *Queer as Folk: Defiinitive Collector's Edition* DVD.

37 See, for instance, the essays collected in Jennifer Doyle, Jonathan Flatley and José Esteban Muñoz (eds) (1996), *Pop Out: Queer Warhol* (Durham, NC, and London: Duke University Press).

38 Antony Cotton, *Queer as Folk: Defiinitive Collector's Edition* DVD commentary, series 1 episode 3.

39 Russell T. Davies (1999), *Queer as Folk: The Scripts* (London: Channel 4 Books), p. 16.

40 For further analysis of the 1990s' mainstreaming of homosexuality in the US, and its problematic politics, see Alexandra Chasin (2000), *Selling Out: The Gay and Lesbian Movement Goes to Market* (New York: Palgrave).

41 Sam Wollaston (1999), 'This Boys' Life – Slick and Snazzy but Rather Lacking Analysis', *Guardian*, 24 February, p. 3.

42 Michael Collins (2000), 'Sing If You're Glad to Be Gay (and Cute)', *Observer*, 'Television' section, 30 January, p. 7.

43 Duncan Marr (2000), 'He's So Nice!', *Gay Times* no. 257, February, p. 23.

44 See Leo Bersani (1996), *Homos* (Cambridge, MA: Harvard University Press), pp. 113–84; Charley Shiveley (1991), 'Indiscriminate Promiscuity as an Act of Revolution', in Winston Leyland (ed.), *Gay Roots: Twenty Years of Gay*

Sunshine (San Francisco, CA: Gay Sunshine Press), pp. 257–63 – Shiveley's essay was fiirst published in 1974.

45 Marr, 'Spunk on the Screen', p. 19.

46 Davies, *Queer as Folk: The Scripts*, p. 8.

47 Margaret E. Johnson (2004), 'Boldly Queer: Gender Hybridity in *Queer as Folk*', *Quarterly Review of Film and Video* vol. 21 no. 4, p. 293.

48 Quoted in Anon (1999), 'No Folk without Fire on 4', *Pink Paper* no. 572, 26 February, p. 1.

49 Quoted in Sanderson, 'There's Nowt So Queer as Hacks', pp. 64, 67.

50 Ibid., p. 67.

51 McKee, 'Interview with Russell T. Davies', pp. 239–40.

52 Glen Creeber (2004), *Serial Television: Big Drama on the Small Screen* (London: BFI, 2004), p. 135.

53 R. Bruce Brassell (1992), 'My Hustler: Gay Spectatorship as Cruising', *Wide Angle* vol. 14 no. 2, pp. 62, 63.

54 Laura Mulvey (1975), 'Visual Pleasure and Narrative Cinema', *Screen* vol. 16 no. 3, pp. 6–18; John Ellis (1982), *Visible Fictions: Cinema, Television, Video* (London: Routledge and Kegan Paul).

55 Lee Edelman (2004), *No Future: Queer Theory and the Death Drive* (Durham, NC, and London: Duke University Press).

56 Davies, *Queer as Folk* DVD commentary, series 1 episode 5.

57 Ibid., series 1 episode 8.

58 Craig Kelly, *Queer as Folk: Defiinitive Collector's Edition* DVD commentary, series 1 episode 5.

59 Davies, *Queer as Folk* DVD commentary, series 1 episode 6.

60 Ibid., series 1 episode 5.

61 Kath Weston (1991), *Families We Choose: Lesbians, Gays, Kinship* (New York: Columbia University Press).

62 Davies, *Queer as Folk: The Scripts*, p. 22.

63 Both quoted in Paul Flynn (1999), 'Queer Street', *Attitude*, January. Article archived at <www.charliehunnam.com.ar>, accessed 20 January 2007.

64 John Caughie (2000), 'What Do Actors Do When They Act?', in Jonathan Bignell, Stephen Lacey and Madeleine Macmurraugh-Kavanagh (eds), *British Television Drama: Past, Present and Future* (Basingstoke: Palgrave), pp. 166–7.

65 Davies, *Queer as Folk: The Scripts*, p. 117.
66 Davies, *Queer as Folk* DVD booklet, p. 11.
67 See Peter Billingham (2000), *Sensing the City through Television* (Bristol: Intellect Books), pp. 119–56.
68 Davies, *Queer as Folk* DVD commentary, series 1 episode 8.
69 Ibid.
70 Robin Nelson (1997), *TV Drama in Transition: Forms, Values and Cultural Change* (London and New York: Macmillan).
71 Dennis Allen (1995), 'Homosexuality and Narrative', *Modern Fiction Studies* vol. 41 nos. 3–4 (Fall–Winter), pp. 609–34.
72 Anna McCarthy (2001), '*Ellen*: Making Queer Television History', *GLQ: A Journal of Lesbian and Gay Studies* vol. 7 no. 4, pp. 593–620.
73 Judith Roof (1996), *Come As You Are: Sexuality and Narrative* (New York: Columbia University Press).
74 Kristin Hohenadel (1999), 'No Tea and Sympathy for Them', *Los Angeles Times*, Home Edition, Calendar Section, 21 November, p. 8.
75 Michael Jackson (1999), 'Four the Record', *Guardian*, Media Guardian, 5 July, p. 3.
76 Ken Tucker (1999), 'The Best and Worst of 1999', *Entertainment Weekly*, 24 December, p. 130.
77 Michael Jackson (1999), 'Chief Executive's Report', in *Television That Matters: Channel 4 Report and Financial Statements 1999*, p. 5. Available online at <www.channel4.com/microsites/F/foia/documents/annual_report_1999.pdf>, accessed 3 February 2007.
78 Davies, *Queer as Folk* DVD booklet, pp. 19–21.
79 Russell T. Davies, *Queer as Folk: The Defiinitive Collector's Edition* DVD commentary for *Queer as Folk 2*, episode 2.
80 Marr, 'Spunk on the Screen', pp. 18–19.
81 Davies, *Queer as Folk* DVD booklet, p. 22.
82 Ibid., p. 23.
83 Bruce LaBruce (1997), *The Reluctant Pornographer* (Toronto: Gutter Press), p. 46.
84 For further discussion of this scene, see Billingham, 'Can Kinky Sex Ever Be Politically Correct?', p. 120, and Sally Munt (2000), 'Shame/Pride Dichotomies in *Queer as Folk*', *Textual Practice* vol. 14 no. 3, p. 538.
85 'Programme Complaints and Intervention Reports', <www.ofcom.org.uk/static/archive/itc/itc_publications/complaints_reports/programme_complaints/show_complaint.asp-prog_complaint_id=269.html>, accessed 20 January 2007.
86 Della Femina (2000), 'The Final Chapter', <www.televisionwithoutpity.com/articles/content/a4580/index-2.html>, accessed 20 January 2007.
87 Alkarim Jivani (1999), preview of *Queer as Folk*, *Time Out* no. 1494, 7–14 April, p. 179.
88 Della Femina (2000), 'Enquiring Minds Want to Know', <www.televisionwithoutpity.com/articles/content/a4582/index-5.html>, 27 October, accessed 20 January 2007.
89 Ibid.
90 Davies, *Queer as Folk* DVD booklet, p. 26.
91 Femina, 'Enquiring Minds Want to Know'.
92 Scott Matthewman (2000), 'Folk off to America – An Interview with Russell T. Davies', <uk.gay.com/printit/entertainment/tv/245>, 30 November, accessed 20 January 2007.
93 Janine Gibson (1999), 'US to Remake Queer as Folk', *Guardian*, 4 October.
94 Ibid.
95 Erich Boehm (1999), 'Channel 4's U.S. Redux' *Variety* vol. 76 no. 7, 4 October, p. 53.
96 Hohenadel, 'No Tea and Sympathy for Them', p. 8.
97 McKee, 'Interview with Russell T. Davies', p. 243.
98 Quoted in Paul Ruditis (2003), *Queer as Folk: The Book* (New York: Pocket Books), p. 105.
99 Joyce Millman, 'The Gayest Story Ever Told', <archive.salon.com/ent/col/mill/2000/11/29/queer_as_folk/index.html>, accessed 17 February 2007.
100 Walter Chaw, review of *Queer as Folk* season 1 DVD, <fiilmfreakcentral.net/dvdreviews/queerasfolk.html>, accessed 17 February 2007.
101 Unauthored poll results, *The Advocate*, June 2006, p. 97. *Queer as Folk US* attained a vote of 56 per cent, Madonna 33 per cent, Cher 30 per cent.
102 Anna McCarthy (2005), 'Crab People from the Centre of the Earth', *GLQ: A Journal of Lesbian and Gay Studies* vol. 11 no. 1, p. 99.
103 Jacques Peretti (2000), 'Only in America', *Guardian*, 12 December.
104 Russell T. Davies (2001), 'A Rose by Any Other Name', *Observer*, 2 September.
105 Quoted in Daniel Martin (2006), 'Jack of Hearts', *Gay Times* no. 337, October, p. 42.

Credits

Queer as Folk
series one

United Kingdom/1999

directed by
Charles McDougall (1–4)
Sarah Harding (5–8)
produced by
Nicola Shindler
written by
Russell T. Davies

©1999
A Red production for Channel 4

1st assistant director
Chris Dando
2nd assistant director
Tom Gabbutt
3rd assistant director
Matthew Greenhalgh
production runner
Ann Iveson
location managers
Sam Taylor (1–4)
Neil Sherry (5–8)
assistant location managers
Frith Tiplady (1–4)
Andrew Swarbrick (5–8)
unit manager
Frith Tiplady (5–8)
script supervisor
Carol Saunderson
production co-ordinator
Tracy Lee
production secretaries
Stephen Walker (1–4)
Eleanor Greene (5–8)
assistant production secretary
Stephen Walker (5)
assistant production co-ordinator
Stephen Walker (6–8)
production office runner
Eleanor Greene (1–4)
post-production assistant
Louise Adamson (8)

unit driver
Robin Davies
dialogue coach
David Johnson (1, 8)
publicity
Joy Sapieka Associates
production accountant
Nicholas Stanley
assistant accountant
Andrew Critchley
casting
David Shaw
additional casting
James Hall (1–4)
Simon Jolly (5–8)
camera operator
Andrew McDonnell (5–8)
focus pullers
Andrew McDonnell (1–4)
Jason Olive (5–8)
clapper loaders
Jason Olive (1–4)
Stuart Chapman (5–8)
camera assistant
Nicholas Walters (6–8)
grip
Alfiie Williams
camera trainee
Stuart Chapman (1–4)
steadicam
Howard J. Smith (1–3)
steadicam operator
Vincent McGahon (6)
boom operators
Justin Wilkinson (1–3)
Garie Kan (4–8)
sound assistant
David Lynch
lighting gaffer
Dave Oldroyd
best boy
Eddie Monaghan (1–5)
electricians
Ben Horsefiield
David Gray
Geoff Latham (6–8)
genny operator
Robert Doe-Wansey

wardrobe supervisor
Emma Rosenthal
wardrobe
Sarah Ryan
make-up supervisor
Lynn Davie
make-up assistant
Alyn Waterman
art director
John Collins
stand-by art director
Cliona Harkin
art department assistant
Jamie Gray
graphic design
Lucy Boyle
production buyer
Jerry Organ
props master
Nigel Salter
stand-by props
Noel Cowell
John Smith
dressing props
Chris Cull
Tom Pleydell-Pearce
construction manager
Steve Bedford
stand-by carpenter
Keith Eccleston
stand-by painter
Mark Roberts
carpenter
Darren Mernagh
action vehicles
Alan Eccleston (3, 4, 6–8)
Cyril White (3, 4, 6–8)
colourist
Neil Parker (3–8)
assistant editors
Chris Clarkson
David Boyle
dialogue editors
John Crumpton (1, 2, 5–8)
Jack Dardis (3, 4)
effects editor
John Rutherford (1, 2, 5–8)
John Crumpton (3, 4)

assistant dubbing editor
Paul Horsfall (3–8)
dubbing mixers
John Whitworth (1–7)
Andy Wyatt (8)
archive
Dangerous to Know (8)
script editor
Matt Jones
casting director
Beverley Keogh
composer
Murray Gold
sound recordist
Gary Desmond
make-up designer
David Jones
costume designer
Pam Tait
editors
Tony Cranstoun (1–4)
Anthony Ham G.B.F.E. (5–8)
director of photography
Nigel Walters B.S.C.
designer
Claire Kenny
associate producer
Tom Sherry
created and co-produced by
Russell T. Davies
executive producer
Nicola Shindler

cast
Aidan Gillen (1–8)
Stuart Jones
Craig Kelly (1–8)
Vince Tyler
Charlie Hunnam (1–8)
Nathan Maloney
Jason Merrells (1, 2, 3)
Phil Delaney
David Prosho (1)
muscle man
Andy Devine (1–8)
Bernard Thomas
Denise Black (1–8)
Hazel Tyler
Saira Todd (1–3, 5–8)
Lisa Levene
Esther Hall (1–8)
Romey Sullivan
Juley McCann (1, 2, 5–8)
Siobhan Potter

Sarah Jones (1, 2, 5–8)
Suzie Smith
Alfred/Alfie Robinson (1–8)
Baby Alfred
Alan Halsall (1, 4)
Midge
Carla Henry (1–8)
Donna Clarke
Ben Maguire (1, 2, 4, 6, 8)
Christian Hobbs

episode two
Paul Simpson
man in toilet
Alison Burrows (2–8)
Sandra Docherty
Susan Cookson (2, 8)
Marcie Finch
Caroline Pegg (2–8)
Rosalie Cotter
Caroline O'Neill (2–8)
Janice Maloney
Jane Cawdron (2, 6, 8)
Helen Maloney
David Williamson
Bob Green
Steve Ramsden
Colin Goodluk

episode three
Adam Zane (3, 7)
Dane McAteer
Antony Cotton (3, 4, 6, 7, 8)
Alexander Perry
Toshi Dokiya
Lee Kane
Richard Slack
threesomes 1
Michael Norris
threesomes 2
Andrew Lancel (3, 8)
Harvey Black
Jim Shepley
Jonathan Walker
Paul Oldham
Spike O'Hagan
Kate Fitzgerald (3, 4)
Mrs Delaney

episode four
Peter O'Brien (4–8)
Cameron Roberts
Caroline Steele
neighbour

episode fiive
Jonathon Natynczyk (5, 6, 7)
Dazz Collinson
Maria Doyle Kennedy (5, 6)
Marie Threepwood
Michael Culkin
Martin Brooks
Jack Deam
Gareth Critchly
John Brobbey (5–8)
Lance Amponah

episode six
Ger Ryan
Margaret Jones
Ian McElhinney
Clive Jones
Paul Copley (6, 8)
Roy Maloney

episode eight
Adam Heywood Fogerty
Roger Clements
Michael Atkinson
Mr Latham
Lee Warburton
striking man
Samantha Cunningham
Cathy Mott
Robert Ashcroft
Gary McGee
Roxy Hart
karaoke hostess

transmission history
episode one Channel 4 tx 23
February 1999 (22.30–23.10)
episode two Channel 4 tx 2
March 1999 (22.30–23.10)
episode three Channel 4 tx 9
March 1999 (22.30–23.10)
episode four Channel 4 tx 16
March 1999 (22.30–23.10)
episode five Channel 4 tx 23
March 1999 (22.30–23.10)
episode six Channel 4 tx 30
March 1999 (22.30–23.10)
episode seven Channel 4 tx 6
April 1999 (22.30–23.10)
episode eight Channel 4 tx 13
April 1999 (22.30–23.15)

133

Queer as Folk 2

United Kingdom/2000

directed by
Menhaj Huda
produced by
Nicola Shindler
written by
Russell T. Davies

©2000
A Red production for Channel 4

1st assistant director
Matt Greenhalgh
2nd assistant director
Deborah Constable
3rd assistant director
Liz Reeve
production runner
Richard Harris
location manager
Terry Reeve
assistant location manager
Frith Tiplady
script supervisor
Kirstie Edgar
production co-ordinator
Tracy Lee
production secretary
Louise Adamson
production office runner
Rachel Marsh
unit driver
Dennis Reid
publicity
Joy Sapieka Associates
still photographer
Jaap Buitendijk (2)
production accountant
Andrew Critchley
assistant accountant
Sue Balmer
assistant casting director
David Shaw
additional casting
Damian Butt
focus puller
Andy Newall
clapper loader
Julie Bills
camera assistant
Joe Maples
grip
Tim Procter

boom operator
Justin Wilkinson
lighting gaffer
Dave Oldroyd
best boy
Peter Brimson
electrician
Ben Horsefiield
genny operator
Jamie Summers
rigger
Dave Grey
wardrobe supervisor
Sarah Moore
costume assistant
Kevin Pollard
dresser
Jo Carlon
costume runner
Kate Laver
make-up supervisor
Sheila Flynn
make-up assistant
Mat Blindell
art director
Paul Gilpin
stand-by art director
Karen Gibbons
assistant art director
Kevin Walker
production buyer
David Lewis
property master
Simon Price
stand-by props
Jason Wood
Rebecca Nevelle
dressing props
Quentin Davies
Dave Ackrill
prop van driver
Martin Lawrence
construction manager
Glen Taylor
stand-by carpenter
Ralph Dronsfiield
stand-by painter
Arthur Orwin
action vehicles
Alan Eccleston
Cyril White
Geoff Kay
Tony Flannery
stunt co-ordinator
Glen Marks

post-production supervisors
Chris Clarkson
David Boyle
editor's assistant
Dave Williams
dubbing editor
Dave Aston
dubbing mixer
Andy Wyatt
post-production effects
MPC
caterers
Little Red Courgette
lighting equipment
Web Lighting
script editor
Matt Jones
composer
Murray Gold
sound recordist
Gary Desmond
make-up designer
Alyn Waterman
costume designer
Michael Johnson
casting director
Beverley Keogh
editor
Tony Cranstoun
production designer
Jeff Tessler
director of photography
Alasdair Walker
line producer
Tom Sherry
created and co-produced by
Russell T. Davies
executive producer
Nicola Shindler

cast
Aidan Gillen
Stuart Jones
Craig Kelly
Vince Tyler
Charlie Hunnam
Nathan Maloney
Denise Black
Hazel Tyler
Antony Cotton
Alexander Perry

episode one
Clinton Kenyon
Mickey Smith

134

James Foster
1st man in sauna
Anthony Collier
2nd man in sauna
Calum Arnott
3rd man in sauna
Susan Cookson (+2)
Marcie Finch
Caroline Pegg (+2)
Rosalie Cotter
Pearce Quigley (+2)
Graham Beck
Maria Doyle Kennedy
Marie Jones
Stuart Mawdsley
Ben Jones
Andrew Maudsley
Thomas Jones
Judy Holt (+2)
Claire Fletcher
Andy Devine (+2)
Bernard Thomas
Roxy Hart (+2)
karaoke hostess
Jonathon Natynczyk
Dazz Collinson
Naomi Radcliffe
Judith Collins
James McClaren
Adrian Collins

Alan Rothwell
Dudley Jackson
Ben Maguire (+2)
Christian Hobbs
Caroline O'Neill (+2)
Janice Maloney
Jane Cawdron
Helen Maloney
Ian McElhinney
Clive Jones
Ger Ryan
Margaret Jones
Olivia K. Critchley (+2)
baby Alfred
Kate Rutter (+2)
Mrs Perry

episode two
Michael Norris
orange spunk man
Stephen Da Costa
toothbrush man
Lee Seddon
snogging man
Julie Armstrong
secretary
Susan McArdle
Sally Rawlins
John Wheeler
John Blake

Malcolm Pitt
teacher
Stephanie Wilmore
1st girl at party
Donna Marie Dawson
2nd girl at party
Liz Wilde
paramedic
Alison Burrows
Sandra Docherty
Jeff Merchant
D.I. Mason
Esther Hall
Romey Sullivan
Mark Ledsham
handsome man
Dave Nicholls
P.C. Stroud
Tony Maudsley
faggot man

transmission history
episode one Channel 4 tx 15
February 2000 (22.00–23.00)
episode two Channel 4 tx 22
February 2000 (22.00–23.00)

135

Index

Page numbers in *italics* refer to illustrations; *n* = endnote

A
Abbott, Paul 4
acting 63–8
Advise and Consent 94
aesthetics 2, 20, 22–31, 34, 39, 52, 85, 115, 118–19
Ali G 83
Allen, Dennis 80
age of consent 20, 39, 87, 90–1
AIDS/HIV 10, 11, 12, 14, 15, 29, 34, 42, 49, 111, 122
Ally McBeal 23
Araki, Gregg 24, 25, 39, 107
Arnott, Jake 128
As If 39

B
Back to the Future 105
Bad Seed, The 93
bars/clubs, representation of 37, 45–8, *46*, 74, 76, 115, *115*
Batman 110
Beadle-Blair, Ricki 127
Beat, Jackie 66
Beautiful Thing 39
Beck's Beer 19
'Big Cock City' (website) 94
blackmail 77, 86, 90, 93–4
Blair, Tony 6
Blondie 24, 45
Bob and Rose 4, 76, 101–2, 125, 126
Bolton Seven 20
Bonnie and Clyde 105
Bound 29
Boy George 13
Boys from the Blackstuff 7
Boys in the Band, The 62
Brassell, R. Bruce 44
Britpop 24–6
Broadcasting Standards Commission 41, 49

Broken Hearts Club, The 61
Brookside 9, 103
Buffy the Vampire Slayer 39
Burchill, Julie 128

C
Cadinot (porn company) 30
Cagney and Lacey 113
camp 17, 57, 65–6, 70, 96–7, 104, 110
Car Wash 110
Casanova 4, 125
Casualty 9, 74
Cathy Come Home 7
Caughie, John 67–8
Century Falls 4, 101
Channel 4, remit of 5–6
Cher 121
Cherry, Marc 101
Children of Men 127
Chitty Chitty Bang Bang 105
Citizen Kane 33
Clarke, Alan 7
Clary, Julian 29
class 16, 17, 29, 50–1, 64, 70, 72, 102
Clause 28/Section 28 75, 88
Clinton, Bill 75
Clocking Off 4, 5, 26, 71, 126
Clone Zone 14, 29
Cold Feet 59, 71
coming out 22, 51, 80–1, 86, 90, 91, 92, 93–6, *95*, 98
Conviction 126
Cops, The 71–2, *73*
Coronation Street 4, 71–2, *71*, 81, 101, 127
Cotton, Antony 26, *60*, *65*, 67, *97*, 127
Countdown 6
Cowen, Ron 111
Cracker 4, 11, 37, 110
Crawford, Cindy 29

credits sequences 26, *27*, 31, *84*, 85, 117–18, *117*
Creeber, Glen 44
Crisp, Quentin 8
cruising 22, 42–5, *43*, 52, 85
Cukor, George 30
Cutting It 71

D
Damned If You Don't 107
Dando, Jill 96–7
Dante's Cove 128
Dark Season 1, 4
Davies, Andrew 128
Davies, Russell T. *5*
    authorial voice 36, 68, 96, 101–2
    career 1, 3–4, 125–6
    relationship with Channel 4 11, 83, 107–9, 110
    writing of *Queer as Folk* 9–12, 15, 16–17, 21, 34–5, 37, 54–5, 72, 83–4, 86–8, 107–8
Dawson's Creek 39
Desperate Housewives 101, 126
Dishes 18
Divine 66, 67, 119
Doctor Who 4, 17, 25, 32, 62, 102, 105, 125, 126
Doom Generation, The 24
drug use 14, 22, 29, 31, 57, 118, 121, 122
Dwek, Rob 110

E
Early Frost, An 111
East Is East 83
EastEnders 9–10, *9*, 14, 80
Eccleston, Christopher 33
Edelman, Lee 49
Ellen 81, 114, 120
Ellis, John 44

Emmerdale 9
Everage, Dame Edna 57

F
Far From Heaven 107
Father Ted 18
Fingersmith 128
Flawless 110
Fowler, Robbie 18
'framily' 59–61, *60*
Frasier 12, 79
Friedkin, William 62
Friedrich, Su 107
Friends 12, 49, 59

G
Gay as Blazes 123, *123*
genre 39, 90, 107
Gillen, Aidan 2, *13*, *23*, *25*,
    34, *35*, 40, *43*, 51, *60*,
    62, *63*, 66, *76*, 83, *89*,
    95, *99*, *102*, 115, 127
Gimme Gimme Gimme 17
Giuliani, Rudy 122
Gless, Sharon 113, *114*
Go Fish 61
Gold, Murray 24, 26, 72, 124
Gordon, Douglas 116
Grand, The 1, *2*, 4, 11, 17, 72
Green Street 127
Greyson, John 112
Grief 66

H
Harding, Sarah 17, 54, 70,
    127
Harvey, Jonathan 17, 39
Haynes, Todd 107
HBO 17, 110, 111, 119
Henry, Carla *69*, 86
Hillsborough 4, 11, 17
HIV/AIDS *see* AIDS/HIV
Holby City 74
Hollinghurst, Alan 128
Hollyoaks: In The City 81
homophobia 6, 75, 86–7, 91,
    116, 122
Huda, Menhaj 85, 127
Human Traffic 45
Hunnam, Charlie *2*, *27*, *35*, 36,
    40, *43*, *60*, 67, *69*, 108,
    115, 127, 129n11

I
In The Pink 5

Independent Television
    Commission (ITC) 19, 97,
    98
Isaacs, Jeremy 129*n*8
Island, The 74

J
Jackson, Michael 10, 82, 83
Jarman, Derek 5
Jones, Matt 16

K
Kath and Kim 57
Keeping Up Appearances 103
Kelly, Craig *2*, *13*, *23*, *32*, *43*,
    48, 55, *56*, *60*, *62*, 67,
    88, *89*, *97*, *99*, 108
Kidulthood 127
Kuchar, George 107

L
L Word, The 128
L. A. Law 23
LaBruce, Bruce 66, 93
Labour Party/'New Labour' 6,
    24, 87
lang, kd 29
Last Temptation of Christ, The 19
Le Saux, Graeme 20
League of Gentlemen, The 17,
    18
Ledsham, Mark 104
lesbians, representation of in
    Queer as Folk 3, 11, 12,
    13, 22, 49, 51–3, 59,
    64–5, 85–6, 118, 120
Linda Green 76, 126
Line of Beauty, The 128
Lipman, Daniel 111, 119
Living End, The 105
Loach, Ken 7
Lonesome Cowboys 107
Long Firm, The 128
Longtime Companion 61
Lost Language of Cranes, The
    40, 45
Love in the 21st Century 110
Love! Valour! Compassion! 61

M
MacKenzie, Catriona 10, 11,
    45, 83
McCarthy, Anna 81, 123
McDougall, Charles 17, 23, 54,
    126

McGovern, Jimmy 4
Made in Britain 7
Madonna 121
'mainstreaming of
    homosexuality' 20, 29–30,
    59, 114–6
Manchester, representations of
    71–4, *73*
Mason, Angela 12
Maupin, Armistead 10
Melrose Place 59, 80
Metrosexuality 127
Michael, George 17, 26
Mine All Mine 4, 22, 26, 125
Minogue, Kylie 24, 45, 57
Misfits 107–9
misogyny in *Queer as Folk* 51,
    52
Mulcahy, Russell 112, 118
Mulvey, Laura 44
My Hustler 44
My Own Private Idaho 105, *106*

N
Naked Civil Servant, The 8, *9*
narrative form 12, 20, 31, 37,
    41, 55, 56, 79–81, 84–5,
    93, 94, 116, 121–2, 124
Natynczyk, Jonathon 67, *69*
Neal, Gub 10, 11, 14, 45, 83,
    110
Neighbours 48, 56
Nelson, Robin 80
New Queer Cinema 16, 24, 39,
    61, 105, 107
Nicholas Nickleby 127
Nighthawks 45, *46*
Noah's Arc 127, 128
Norton, Graham 29
Nowhere 24, *25*, 107

O
Office, The 127
Our Friends in the North 4
Out/Out on Tuesday 6
OutRage! 16, 36, 102
Owen, Wilfred 75, 76, 91
Oz 119

P
parents, relationships with 58,
    66, 90, 96–102
Parkinson 17
Paris is Burning 61
Peter's Friends 59

Phoenix Nights 71
Podeswa, Jeremy 112
pop art 24
Poptastic (club) 25–6
'positive images' 3, 14–15, 53, 91
Potter, Dennis 4, 126
Prime Suspect 4, 11
Prisoner Cell Block H 57
Prowler 29

Q

'queer', history of term 15–16
Queer Duck 16
Queer Eye for the Straight Guy 16, 123, 124
queer family 57–61, 98
  see also 'framily'
Queer Nation 16
queer parenting 6, 36, 49, 61, 122
  see also queer family
Queercore 16, 24

R

race/ethnicity 12, 16, 29, 30, 39, 51–2, 90, 91–3, 121
realism 2, 24, 30, 66–7, 74–5, 96, 121
Reality Bites 60
Red Production Company 4–5, 26, 110, 126
Rich, B. Ruby 16, 107
Roof, Judith 81
Royle Family, The 71

S

Sarah Jane Adventures, The 126
Savage, Lily 29
scheduling 18, 42, 84

Schumacher, Joel 110, 111
Scorsese, Martin 19
Second Coming, The 4, 5, 26, 85, 108–9
Sex and the City 17–18, 41–2, 101, 119, 127
sex scenes 3, 10, 13, 22, 38–42, *40*, 83, 119–20, *120*
Sexual Offences (Amendment) Bill 19–20, 87
  see also age of consent
Shameless 4, 26, 71, 72, *73*, 80
Shepard, Matthew 17, 88
Shindler, Nicola 4–5, 10, 17, 23, 45, 51, 83, 84, 108, 126
Showcase 111, 121
Showtime 3, 111, 119, 121, 128
Simpsons, The 130n30
Singing Detective, The 107
Sisters 111
Six Feet Under 59, *60*
Soap! 107
soap opera 4, 9, 16, 56, 71, 72, 80, 121, 124
Sopranos, The 119
soundtrack 2, 24–9, 118–19
South Bank Show, The 129n7
Spall, Timothy 77
Spooks 31
Springfield, Dusty 20
Star, Darren 17, 101
State of Play 4
stereotypes 8, 13, 15, 64–6
  see also positive images
Stonewall 12, 36, 102
Sugar Rush 128
Super 8 ½ 66

T

Tales of the City 10
teenagers 36, 39, 90
Thatcher, Margaret 75
Thelma and Louise 105
thirtysomething 59, 107
This Life 2–3, 10, 11, 59, 85
Tipping the Velvet *126*, 127
Titanic 113
Torchwood 125, 126
*Totally F***ed Up* 39, 61
Trainspotting 45
Trash 66
24 Hour Psycho 116
Twin Peaks 107

U

Undeclared 127

V

Victim 94

W

Wainwright, Rufus 30
*Wallpaper** (magazine) 28, 94
Warhol, Andy 44, 61, 66, 107
Warren, Tony 101
Waters, Sarah 127
Weston, Kath 59
Will and Grace 59, 114, 128
Wintour, Anna 101
Wire, The 127
Woodlawn, Holly 66

Y

Young Americans 127
Young, Baroness 87
Young Person's Guide to Being a Rock Star, The 110